Manifesto of the New Economy

Alexander Dolgin

Manifesto of the New Economy

Institutions and Business Models of the Digital Society

Springer

Professor Alexander Dolgin
Moscow State School of Economics
Bolshaya Akademicheskaya Str. 5
Moscow
Russia
adolgin@imhonet.ru

Translated by Arch Tait

ISBN 978-3-642-21276-5 e-ISBN 978-3-642-21277-2
DOI 10.1007/978-3-642-21277-2
Springer Heidelberg Dordrecht London New York

Library of Congress Control Number: 2011933467

Printed on acid-free paper

Springer is part of Springer Science+Business Media (www.springer.com)

Contents

Chapter 1
Introduction

A spectre is haunting the globe – the spectre of the New Economy, a phenomenon for which a definitive name has yet to be found and which for now is hidden behind an uninformative signboard. We are going to take a look at it, to see which human practices, already established or still in the making, characterise it, and which of its tools and institutions hold out most promise.

Many have little enthusiasm for the lifestyle the New Economy has visited upon us. They see it in terms of the deficiencies of mass culture, as emphasising inequalities between people even as it levels down and eradicates the uniqueness of cultures all over the planet. This is difficult to counter. The New Economy brings much that is of value, but even if this is conceded the value it brings is considered shallow and trivial. There is general agreement that the pluses are far from compensating for the minuses. But before deciding whether to condone or condemn the changes it brings, let us take a closer look at its arrangements and give more thought to its ethical dimension.

Let us start by seeing what traditional economic science has to say about it. Much of life is linked to markets, which is why our everyday reality is more accessible to economists than to other social scientists. There is much to be learned from prices and the volume of goods being produced. With the assistance of money the sheer variety of life can be turned into numbers, to enter the jurisdiction of mathematics, and thence proceed to the planners to be administered. Where economic modelling proves successful we can derive a summary vector, the overall resultant of social forces, the thing that turns the millstones of history on the grand (and on a more intimate) scale.

Often, however, we are dealing with a complex, motile, incalculable system of forces which derive from the motivations of groups with differing interests. Although methodologies have been devised to deal with this, more often than not

A. Dolgin, *Manifesto of the New Economy*,
DOI 10.1007/978-3-642-21277-2_1,

it is anyone's guess which vector is going to prevail and which direction the ship of state will move in. The result is that much reliance is placed on political intuition, and decisions are taken on the basis of guesswork and hoping for the best. With their schemes of classification, economists do sometimes predict correctly how things will develop, although since the financial crisis they have been looked at askance. There are complaints that they failed to sound the alarm and have yet to come up with a solution. Well, the current standing of economics is not our main concern but it does conveniently lead on to discussion of the New Economy (which could equally well have started from the adverse selection which bedevils cultural markets).

If the general public take the view that economists have dug themselves into a hole, at least that did not result from professional incompetence. Factors they don't monitor rebelled, forces which they know about in the abstract but which current systems for measuring markets can't take proper account of, which economic philosophy doesn't fully understand and therefore leaves out of its calculations. These, for traditional economics, exogenous factors are linked to metamorphoses occurring in the soul of well-fed homo sapiens. Economists don't do a bad job of modelling a hungry man, particularly if he is a European and not too hungry. They are doing much less well in trying to get the measure of homo sapiens when he is enjoying a high level of material satisfaction.

Economists are ignorant of anything outside the domain of the market so they classify it as being of no importance, which means they get their sums seriously wrong. They are often uneasily aware, or at least suspect, that these unknown quantities exist, but what can they do? When society suddenly becomes unpredictable, we know we have entered a danger zone. Much of what is missed by traditional economics – people's motivations, desires and moods, their cognitive resources of memory and attention, the speed of their mental reactions, their cultural codes and values, their aesthetic tastes and so on, which have hitherto been seen as aspects of the psyche and hence the province of social psychology, now come within the purview of the New Economics. The aim of the present book is to show how we can uncover these unknowns and put them to work for the good of society. How are we best to access and process this under-researched knowledge about ourselves and the world around us, which we all have but which we keep to ourselves?

As primarily an information economics, the New Economics is well suited to the job of looking directly at the individual human being. Particular attention is going to be paid, then, to interpersonal communications, primarily on the internet, an environment where many novelties are born. We are going to look at a new way for people to interact, and specifically at a new way for them to cooperate, through collaborative filtering. This is something currently familiar mainly to professionals and advanced internet users, but it is extremely important for the New Economy and the information society as a whole.

Collaborative filtering, which is essentially group filtering, is a system for exchanging subjective experience. It makes it possible to choose objects and information which can be expected to appeal to the tastes and preferences of each individual member of a group. The idea behind it is that groups of like-minded individuals can be built up on the basis of judgements by a large number of people of the quality of whatever interests them. Their judgements can be registered, for example, by means of rating. Within their group information will be exchanged which will make it possible to use the judgements of certain group members to predict how other group members will respond to goods they have yet to experience. The principle is similar to word of mouth, except that it has been automated and purged of "noise." Confidence in the value of new recommendations is based on the experience of past success. If one of the group members is the first to find out about something interesting, he can assess it, inform the others, and save them the trouble of each individually repeating the assessment. They in turn may discover something of general interest and reciprocate. Collaborative filtering is really just a universal mechanism for consumer testing the quality of all manner of things: goods, texts, works, – even people. It is indispensable for a society which is being overwhelmed by superabundance. Collaborative filtering, for all its novelty, is only replicating the way anybody acts when faced with the need to make a choice: find someone sensible who has been in the same situation and ask them what they think. Computerising this kind of action was a really major achievement of the turn of the millennium, and the scope of the discovery and the areas to which collaborative filtering can be applied has yet to be appreciated.

People are in constant contact with other people in many connections, and with which people and in which connections underlie the quality of their life. Collaborative filtering is a universal method which enables them to optimise the way they make these links. It facilitates access to knowledge dispersed in society, including our knowledge about each other, and out of this a whole spectrum of institutions, rules and standards can grow to reorganise the way people relate to each other and bring about an overall improvement in the life of society. The quality of our contacts depends on how society divides into groups and on which of them we are capable of belonging to. Much, perhaps everything, in today's society depends on overt or covert stratification, and that is something to which collaborative filtering is ideally suited.

We shall discuss these issues in three sections: (1) analysis of the fundamental problems and logical options for developing the information society; (2) practical institutional planning to find ways of solving the problems that raises; (3) analysis of examples, including a website which provides a platform for networking and collaboration. Thus we will cover the topic from its basic premises to its implementation in practice. Metaphorically speaking, our task is not merely to describe the laws of aerodynamics, but to show how an aircraft can fly, and then show one, created in accordance with the laws of aerodynamics, rising from the runway to demonstrate convincingly the reality of flight.

Chapter 2
The Second Invisible Hand of the Market

2.1 What is the New Economy?

Both the New Economy itself and the lifestyle to which it gives rise are inextricably linked with texts (in the broadest sense of the word): with their production, distribution and consumption. On this basis it is defined as an information economy. A detailed analysis of the New Economy would call for a separate extensive treatise which would only distract us from our topic, so we will restrict ourselves to trying to establish its main distinguishing features.

One of the obvious features of the New Economy has been the preceding growth of costs associated with information processing (so-called transaction costs) as against expenditure on the physical manufacture of goods (transformation costs). Institutional economics has long been familiar with the concept of transaction costs (Ronald Coase). They occur all over the place and relate to all manner of agreements, coordination and interpretation, but like friction they are inconspicuous and difficult to register even when great efforts are made to do so. In the few attempts made to measure them (one was undertaken by Douglass North) about 40% of all expenditure in the business environment was found to be of this kind. Today the figure is probably even higher since the proportion of costs spent creating and processing information is constantly rising. Oddly enough, no one has ever tried to calculate the retail end user's costs. This is not to say that the lawsuits resulting from transaction costs have finally become more significant than the extraction of hydrocarbons or the crop yields of wheat, but, bearing in mind their importance, we can safely say they have been under-researched and underestimated.

The next key characteristic of the New Economy is the sharp increase in the proportion of non-material, non-utilitarian goods in the structure of consumption. These include not only media consumption, not only the realm of culture (cinema,

A. Dolgin, *Manifesto of the New Economy*,
DOI 10.1007/978-3-642-21277-2_2, © The Author(s) 2012

literature, music), which is natural, but also, without exception, every aspect of everyday life which until not long ago was considered to be, and was, utilitarian.

Objects are increasingly used not merely as possessions with useful properties, but as signs, symbols, cultural codes – in brief, as signals and messages. Consuming goods, a person enters into relations with other people: people communicate through their possessions. This process of a large-scale move from utility to symbolism accelerated about half a century ago and was identified by such theoreticians of consumer society as Georges Bataille, Jean Baudrillard, Pierre Bourdieu and Roland Barthes. At that time the new lifestyle was only beginning to appear and their works were prophetic. Now these processes have become so evident that they show up in statistics. That is why now we can and must move from political economics to applied economics, with laws and formulae which enable us to anticipate the course of events. This, indeed, is one of this book's tasks: to identify data which the economics of the New Economy can operate with, and to indicate how they can be collected.

But let us return to the differences between the New Economy and the old. In parallel to changes in the structure of consumption, which is becoming increasingly diverse, individual, and sophisticated, there is a change in the correlation between production and commerce. It is becoming cheaper to manufacture than to sell. The proportion of factory costs in the retail price of goods is decreasing. In several industries the retail price is five or even ten times more than the production cost, and a two to three times markup is almost standard. The markup is determined by costs associated with delivering goods to the retail customer, and a substantial part of these relate to information. Commerce earns its cut legitimately by creating information about demand. A large increase in the retail price over the factory gate cost is a reliable indicator that a particular industry is in the camp of the New Economy. It also indicates unambiguously that the new "information" economy is not confined to the media and entertainment, or to the cultural industries (which include the internet). It also includes such traditional segments of the market as clothing, furniture, electronic household appliances and cars which, despite their thoroughly material appearance, nowadays belong to the information industries and are functioning in accordance with the rules of the New Economy.

We can also list signs of the New Economy which are in strict accordance with traditional economic logic. For example, goods cease to be used long before they have actually worn out. Moral depreciation has overtaken physical depreciation. Possessions are not fully used and could carry on in service for a long time, but are written off because they are out of fashion. They become not just unusable but positively damaging since they discredit their owner in the eyes of those around him. Another sign of the times is that in the past the value of most goods could be assessed fairly accurately by such attributes as weight, size and power. Now products are migrating en masse to the category of "experience goods" which have to be used before you can tell whether they are what you are looking for. Take the mobile telephone. All its features and specifications are described in the bulky instruction booklet, but they vary so much that it is simpler just to buy the telephone and work them out through use. We need not go into this too deeply, but merely note that a key peculiarity of the New Economy is a lack of transparency, a lack of clarity as to the quality of goods, and this result from their sheer numbers and complexity. This leads to "information asymmetry" between what manufacturers know and what consumers can tell, and to distortions of the market when the purchaser is misled. In theory a customer could work out the reality of the situation in each individual case, but he simply hasn't the time to do that for everything. George Akerlof has shown that if the consumer cannot accurately assess the quality of a product, a tendency to "adverse selection" results in inferior goods and services crowding out those which are better. This has brought about a change in how firms compete in the market. They do their utmost to differentiate their wares, to become monopolists in a specific sub-species of a product. In the process the difference is sometimes no more than using a different label and charging a different price. Differentiating everything from everything else makes it possible to avoid having to compete in one large market championship and instead to rule supreme in some cosy niche, thus moving towards the "monopolistic competition" described by Edward Chamberlin.

The next feature of the New Economy is that the price of goods increasingly reflects a personal, situational value refracted through the perception of other people rather than some universal value. This is a consequence of the fact that consumption increasingly resembles collecting. We are talking here not about the collecting of old-fashioned knick-knacks, but a practice embraced by everybody who seeks to position themselves in society by visually presenting facets of their personality. In this game a particular purchase, in the context of a lifestyle, is of interest mainly as the culmination of a series of declaratory purchases which aim to project a desired image.

Without this last purchase, everything previously acquired might be of little value, but it acts rather like that particular condiment which transforms just food into a signature dish. This is why when we are looking at consumption characteristic of the middle and upper storeys of Abraham Maslow's pyramid of needs (where someone's greatest need is for recognition, self-assertion and revelation of their personality), Heinrich Gossen's law of diminishing marginal utility, which is a fundamental of economics, no longer operates. This law points out that each successive portion of a good is less valuable than the one preceding it. It is valid for homogeneous goods in short supply, the need for which is dictated by biological necessity, but it holds no sway in the New Economy because there goods are neither homogeneous nor in short supply. Economists of the past, in particular Wiener, knew of exceptions to Gossen's law and pointed out that goods with network or group effects, like telephones or fashion clothing, had paradoxically increasing utility because their value is tied to the number of users. In the past these really were exceptions, but today network and group effects predominate. Neither does Gossen's law hold for consumption linked to such personal investments as listening to music or creative growth generally, as Gary Becker has pointed out. It might seem that, taking the unit of consumption as being not a single purchase but the collection in its entirety, the law of diminishing marginal utility would again operate, but this view too is untenable because collections are never definitive and there is an endless variety of communities in which they can be displayed.

This is the essential nature and the driver of present-day consumerism. A bought item supplements an existing collection but never finally completes it. In itself it may not be expensive, but the increase in value which it brings to the set is disproportionately large. Anticipating that future gain, the consumer is more tractable, a fact of which the seller is well aware, allowing the price to walk on a long leash. A designer accessory whose factory price is little more than $10 may be put on the shelf with a three-digit price tag. This "scissors effect," where the cost of manufacture diverges wildly from the retail price, is exposed when the price can be slashed during sales. That is the norm in the New Economy.

The distinctive features of the New Economy are a response to fundamental changes in the traditional economy and, of course, in technology. The time structure of our lives is changing, as are the things we do and the length of time we do them for. The number of hours you have to work to satisfy life's basic requirements is decreasing, so one would expect leisure time to increase. This does not always occur, of course, because people may prefer to work more in order to clamber up the social ladder. Nevertheless, the increase in leisure time is very large, not a matter of mere percentage points. In the second place, the quality of work time is changing, perhaps for the better, perhaps not. From a burdensome chore, work may be transformed into personal self-assertion and inspired creativity. On the other hand, it may remain monotonous and tedious and blunt the acuity of the person doing it. Liberation from the rigours of the workplace does not automatically ensure a happy life for the peoples of the world, and even if matters do improve, there is no guarantee that this will be perceived. Finally, the quality of leisure changes, and here too there is no guarantee that it changes for the better when we are less busy. The industrialisation and standardisation of recreation lower its value and attractiveness. For all that, these changes have in common a tendency for the quality of an individual's personal time to rise.

High-quality personal time is time which people themselves rate as having been well spent. A prerequisite is for the individual to have freedom to choose and to use all his abilities to the full. The mission of the New Economy is to bring humanity closer to that ideal.

The concept of quality time is central to this book and it is worth now considering ideas of progress. The ideal of progress has so often led to disappointment, has become so encrusted with connotations of war and global tragedy, that people seem to have quite given up on it. Nevertheless, progress never went away, it was still there, only doubts were ever-increasing as to whether it was actually a blessing. I believe progress can be rehabilitated if we understand it to mean increasing people's quality time. We shall discuss this in Chap. 3.

Economists are in a difficult, even a ticklish situation. The realities of the New Economy are suffused with the symbolic, yet traditional economists continue to operate with material, earthbound bean counting, paying scant attention to the "semiosphere," the changes in people's motivations and the structure of their values. Yet the trends in these areas are so powerful that before you know it they will demolish traditional notions of society, and perhaps society itself. Culture influences the economy, but in the process is increasingly subject to the laws of economics. One might imagine that languages, symbols and signs are born and live in accordance with rules which have little in common with the material economy, and at one time that was true. But even as we watch they are going the same way as air and water, which are beginning to be scarce. They have moved from the category of free goods to the category of economic goods in short supply.

What is it in this subtle, incorporeal matter that has become a resource? On the one hand, it is the signs, works, linguistic and other symbolic constructions themselves. It is increasingly difficult to find a title for something, for example a website, without discovering to your dismay that the combination of letters you fancy has already been appropriated by somebody else. Words and names have become commodities in the most literal sense. They have to be bought for cash from cyber-squatters. That might seem an insignificant symptom, but far more telling is the fact that Google's search system really took off only when they found a way of selling, believe it or not, words. A business pays Google for a word or combination of words, and is thereby enabled to advertise through the search system. In response to users' enquiries containing the relevant words, the business's advertisement appears on the pages of search results.

Far more conspicuously than the accumulation of signs, another problem is becoming evident: the limited nature of such human resources as leisure, attention, memory, emotions and taste. The media and entertainment industries ramp up their offerings but encounter a shortage of eyes and ears. Advertising markets calculate the monetary equivalent of attention, how much a unit of time of a particular social stratum is worth at a particular hour of the day on a particular advertising platform. Production of the symbolic has always been an economic process, if with special features, but now consumption of the symbolic has also become an economic process. Not only people and businesses, but states compete for cultural territory. Take, for example, the battle over which language should be used for encoding the contents of national libraries. Google favours English, while France champions French.

There is another problem, with which possibly we should start since it presents a major challenge to the whole of the theory and practice of economics. Traditionally economics has busied itself with scarcity, distributing resources in short supply in accordance with certain criteria. When dealing with material production, the focus on scarcity makes sense, but to a large extent the New Economy is dealing with non-material products, and thanks to digital technologies the cost of producing them falls virtually to zero. Under these circumstances it is difficult to give scarcity such a central role. What scarcity is there in an electronic file? The carpet is pulled from under the feet of classical economics, although in fact scarcity has not gone away. It has decamped from the phase of production to the phase of consumption, and is ultimately bound up with the receptive capacity of man. If we are to engage seriously with the New Economy, economics has no option but to create a counting system for anthropological resources. An institutional innovation described in this book helps us to find the solution.

2.2 Consumption as Language or, Why Does Society Need Diversity?

The New Economy is an economy of groups whose purpose is to satisfy a person's need for quality communication. This understanding of the current situation is fundamental to all the ideas and thoughts put forward in the present volume. A particular individual's quality of life depends on the kind of people he has around him and on the nature of his interaction with them. It is good to have access to circles in which you (a) acquire necessary contacts, (b) enjoy good standing, and (c) find common interests and a suitable field for activity. This is the area in which the New Economy operates, organising and providing content for groups, communities, and communication clubs. The group is the key unit of consumer society, its end and its means. The entire system of signs, texts and signals is, on the one hand, a means of gaining admission to groups in which a certain kind of person is welcome and another is not; and, on the other hand, it is an information menu for consumption there.

The quality of a group is related to the size and balance of its membership. The group should have neither too many nor too few members. An optimal size will emerge which can be sustained. The information economy and its industries works to produce signs and texts which make possible the successful formation of groups. Dress code at social events is a simple and effective means of regulating who comes in. Something similar, in a more or less sophisticated and veiled way, applies to all groups. Anybody who has not made the effort to learn the conventions or who does not know the passwords (which may be knowledge of particular texts and coded terms) is excluded. The need for visual signals, which can be read instantly and make it possible to stratify society, is what drives the fashion industries. Accessories perform the same function: mobile phones, gadgets, cars and other possessions.

These categories are very eloquent and announce the status and style of consumption you have achieved: how you dress, where your children go to school, what kind of car you drive, what kind of house you live in, how many languages you speak, and the like. All the components of the collection are balanced in terms of price and, more subtly, taste. If one link in the chain is altered, for example, if you take a step up the ladder, all the other links need to follow if a person is not to create an unfavourable impression. If you move up to a more prestigious car, you need to change the kind of clothes you wear.

What sort of nonsense is this, you may ask. Why should a serious person care what kind of superficial impression he creates. If he is a model, fair enough, but otherwise why give a damn about people who judge him by the clothes he wears? It will hardly affect the opinion of people who matter. We will not dwell on this error but confine ourselves to suggesting that the strategy of jackets with holes in the elbows is an alternative form of demonstrative consumption, only with a negative sign. It works to some extent for a very small group of people (for example, eccentric professors) who, as luck would have it, are the people who articulate the principle for everybody else.

The habitus we show the outside world is a public photograph of our social status which, to some degree, also characterises our inner world. Like a bird's plumage it allows a rapid initial filtering of individuals on whom it is not worth wasting time. It makes sense to subject those remaining to closer scrutiny, to listen to what they have to say, what they think, what they have read, how they live their lives. Accordingly, sophisticated consumption is not a whim or a sign of moral depravity, but a rational means of stratifying and dividing to create communities. Every time a person selects and purchases an item, he decides where and in what respects he wants to resemble people who interest him, and in what respects he wishes to differentiate himself from them in order to demonstrate his individuality. He needs to integrate in order to be accepted as an equal, but also to differentiate himself in order to be recognised as an interesting person and to occupy a condign position in the group. Integrating and differentiating oneself are the principal axes of the coordinates of social life, enabling people to position themselves through consumer choice. By demonstrating his taste and talents, each person in society minimises personal costs of time, attention and emotion to establish quality links. Cognitive markers help to minimise communication with unsuitable, "wrong" people. The industries of the New Economy thus produce not mere goods with utilitarian qualities, but primarily a system of signs and signals essential for the ordering of personal life, acquisition of professional contacts, and discovering proximate and less closely related groups. A person needs to belong not just to one group but to several, and on different levels, depending on the diversity of his interests and the facets of his personality. If we reduce the variety of goods, there will be fewer differentiated groups and their membership will be less compatible. People will get on each other's nerves.

2.2.1 *The Ethics of Consumer Society*

Before we conclude this whirlwind tour of the New Economy, we need to look at the ethical aspect of what is taking place. We all live in the world of the New Economy and consume its goods. Whether we are living well or badly depends on each person's circumstances, and these are by no means invariably determined by the economy. Nevertheless, many thoughtful people are instinctively opposed to the New Economy. The place of ostentatious consumption in the prevailing lifestyle grates with them, the lack of respect for the utility of goods and, by implication, for the labour which went into making them, the escalating inequality when some are wallowing in luxury while others can barely make ends meet, and the former couldn't care less, and much else besides. At the risk of inviting opprobrium, we will allow ourselves a few words in praise of the New Economy.

The consumer society does indeed indulge the whims of its relatively successful members. They do devote considerable energy to swallowing up and destroying. Most analysts use the word "consumerism" disparagingly and can see no merit in it. But let us take a different look at the situation, perhaps through the eyes of Bataille who writes of the "accursed share" which has to be destroyed in order to be able to produce more. Rising productivity of labour has freed time which needs somehow to be utilised. The problem of keeping usefully employed in the leisure era has become so acute that the classic Russian question, "What is to be done?" has taken on a new resonance: what is to be done not in the usual sense of "How do we get out of this pickle?" but "How do we keep ourselves occupied?" It is more and more difficult for people to find a productive use for themselves, especially in the technical, engineer's, progressivist sense in which that was previously understood. If work is not dictated by the necessity of earning one's daily bread and a person still feels a need to do something useful, they have to try to think up something to do. In contrast with the previous naturalness of life, this is what is found most exasperating of all: the artificiality, the laboured nature of what is going on.

The New Economy is called an economy of desires, in contrast to the economy galvanised by necessity. That word "desires" tends to be pronounced with a negative inflection, a degree of contempt, as if one is speaking about something primitive and depraved of which one should be ashamed and certainly should not be indulging. If in the past there were grounds for that kind of attitude, today desires deserve to be treated with more respect. The concern is not how society will feed itself, but how it will motivate and busy itself in order not to turn sour. The New Economy is an answer to the problem of motivation and engagement. It was, if you like, invented as an answer to this problem, as a method of utilising activity unproductively, activity liberated from the restricted economy. From a humane viewpoint everything seems fine: the New Economy gives people freedom to do what they want, to communicate with whoever they want and about whatever they want. Humanity has long dreamed of being free, and does not that mean freedom to choose goods and services, lifestyle, how we spend our time, and to join associations which accord with our interests? To put it simply, the right to work and play as we please (although freedom of this kind comes at a price, and you have to pay to belong to the association which interests you). You would suppose that people would have been delighted to enjoy this kind of freedom, and yet the majority spend their time nit-picking and exaggerating the drawbacks. Their praise had been for freedom in the abstract, without understanding its implications, and in their hearts people cannot bear the reality. It has to be said, though, that in the past today's critics were largely paying lip-service to social rhetoric.

Suppose we concede that the consumer really is spoiled, falls far short of the standards of progressive mankind, acts to the detriment of the environment and those around him. His freedom as a consumer is nevertheless also the freedom of a producer! The new markets have performed a miracle by finding work for everyone (or almost everyone) at the same time as entertaining them. Production and consumption are meshed as intimately as two cogwheels. Stop one and you stop the other. Say no to consumption and at the far ends of the earth some luckless fellow for whom we all express much demonstrative concern will lose his job. If we proscribe the predilection of one group of individuals for expensive watches, Hermes bags, cosmetic procedures and similar excesses, we deprive another far more numerous group of jobs. Fulminating against inequalities in the standard of living, we risk breaking the tow rope by which the leaders draw the laggards. We are full of sympathy but do not ourselves know how to compel the rich to share with the poor, unless by force. Critics of the consumer society pretend they have at the ready some other method for the benign redistribution of wealth. Yet the disparaged hyperconsumption is a kind of charity, if in disguise. Where, we need to ask, do those 4/5 of the retail price go which are paid above the factory cost for all manner of baubles and indulgences? Designers, craftsmen and apprentices of every description, service and commercial staff and a horde of creative and working people are fed through this means by the well-off.

The backlash against consumption results from a failure to understand how the new reality operates, and in particular an underestimate of its driving force, human desires. Motivation is a resource which needs to be treated gently. If we disrupt the active part of society's favourite game of stratification, for which money is required, then we may well find these people lose interest in earning money. And that will be bad news for everyone. We will very quickly find out why apparently needless variety is in fact needed. The downturn would not be long in coming. The factory of desires would close and everything would be blown away.

Consumer variety is not a sop but the central nerve of social development. The supply of new goods and the demand for them are crucial processes in today's world. The former enhances the quality of work, and the latter the quality of leisure. People would have nothing to do and life would be very boring if new things were not produced and consumed. For some reason people forget about the reverse side of consumption, work. For a time crises put everything back in perspective, as occurred in 2008. Many who were obliged then to wind down felt keenly how important work is for happiness, and how burdensome the gaps in time are when you don't know what to fill them with. You would imagine that was just the moment to get down to all those things you had been putting off: self-improvement, fitness, children… but you can't be bothered. Work and leisure are like interconnecting vessels: if the level of satisfaction falls in one, the level will fall in the other too.

There are of course solid grounds for giving present-day culture a kicking. Under the influence of commerce the cultural landscape is becoming dull and faded. A complex, intelligent text loses its public and you can't earn a living from it. Creative people adapt themselves to mass demand and subordinate themselves to manufacturers. It would not be difficult to list quite a few dangerous symptoms and distortions which arise as a result of commercialisation and adverse selection of culture. No amount of lamentation and entreaty will deflect the cultural process from the highway along which the popular masses are pushing it, having now discovered how much more gratifying it is to be a creator yourself, rather than merely appreciating the works of other artists, even if they are more skilled.

Industry has gone along with this trend, which it find profitable, levelling down qualification. Electronic sound enables non-professionals to compose music, computer graphics initiate them into design, the blogosphere has made every Tom, Dick and Harriette a writer, and a digital camera has made them a photo- or video-chronicler, if not quite a director. Such a complete move away from being a spectator to amateur creativity is not without consequences, which upset those who cherished the old ways, but this is no excuse for ignoring its major achievement. As we have said, and will yet repeat, the New Economy generates a language, a semiotic system which is essential for high-quality communications, and the latter is the main prerequisite of happiness.

2.3 The Imperative of Conspicuous Consumption

The processes which are perversely interpreted as bad taste, shopaholism and exhibitionism are by no means reducible to that, as the economist Thorsten Veblen made clear a century ago. He spotted that the leisured classes were consuming not goods, but the price of goods, and more precisely its effect on those around them. According to Veblen, what really mattered was not a good's utility but the signal it gave out about the amount paid for it. That is pure information economics logic! Veblen, brought up in the traditions of conspicuous frugality, had little liking for the rich and this comes through in his writings. He had an intellectual understanding of the meaning of conspicuous consumption, but was personally nauseated by it. What hope is there, then, for those who reject cultural trends without having even a theoretical grasp of how the consumer society is arranged?

Expenditure for display has been around from the earliest times, and it is as naive to see it as no more than vacuous strutting as it is to deny the meaningfulness of any other persistent social practice. Leaders of all descriptions, prospering merchants and factory owners, the military and lawyers have all from time to time had recourse to non-functional expenditure. They were not indulging their caprices but acting entirely soberly, creating an impression they needed for their work with the aid of an entourage and, where necessary, expansive gestures.

There is an ulterior motive when a person buys some exotic foreign frippery and dresses his life's companion in it, and there is good reason why he decides to throw a banquet. Through gestures such as these he gains a reputation, and what is the problem if in the process some modicum of satisfaction comes his way too? Those around are persuaded that it will not be easy for him to part with his reputation and this is precisely what he is seeking: a public insurance against the possibility that in the future he might behave in an unseemly manner. The demonstrative expenditure works as a pledge of predictability and a foundation for trust on the part of potential partners. Incidentally, image advertising is also based on the logic of a pledge: anybody whose output of goods is not guaranteed to be of high quality is hardly going to spend a lot of money publicising them. After all, if a rubbish product is made recognisable, it is likely to be more rather than less difficult to sell. Purchasers interpret this signal at a subconscious level. Such is the fundamental logic of expenditure as propitiation. It only seems unnecessary. In fact, it is an investment in information about the future, in trust. It is surprising how little this mechanism is understood, given that it largely governs the behaviour of human beings in general and trade in particular. We should mention here work in the 1960s to 1980s on the information economy, particularly by Michael Spence, and on game theory by Thomas Shelling and Robert Aumann, although knowledge of their work has not yet made it outside a narrow circle of specialists.

Status expenditure is almost an imperative for an overwhelming majority of members of society. It gives a very precise indication of who is who and whether a person is worth paying attention to. The logic of status has been around for a long time, but in the past was most noticeable among the upper crust of society. It caused expensive clothes to be made for the elite, jewellery, accessories, items of interior decor, and was a driver of the economy. Less elaborate items were targeted at the middle strata, while those in the lower ranks of society simply could not afford variety. The class diktat in respect of clothing was needed for purposes which today are achieved more easily, – to make it immediately evident who was who. Since Veblen's time the economic yoke has become less onerous and the game of conspicuous consumption can now be played by all. What is involved is no longer just property-owning status but multiple characterisations of personality. All strata of society are drawn at their own level into the production and reading of the same codes and semiotic crosswords as the well-heeled.

Every level of aspiration has its minimum of consumption. From the most mass produced and cheapest products, beer and chips and football, to music, internet surfing, movies and computer games, everything is done to make it possible to find things to do with available time and to escape its intolerable slowness. Those seeking promotion to a higher league have every opportunity, it is entirely up to the individual. In this we see a humane levelling of opportunity and a satisfying of all types of demand, tastes and ambitions by consumer culture. The system artfully brings people together or differentiates them, as a result of which the various classes, layers, strata, circles and segments of society are delicately accommodated and less likely to cause serious injury to each other with their sharp elbows. That is why being snooty about somebody else's popcorn, for example, is to fail to recognise that it is enabling you to distinguish your kind of people from the rest (or to make a big thing of your knowledgeability).

We have reached a point where contemporary society is increasingly managed by a rational symbolic code no less powerful than competition for material resources. This engenders different realities and a different morality to go with them which it would be mistaken to judge from the old standpoint. Below we analyse how this mechanism of the information economy operates.

2.4 Personal Thoughts

Human beings can do all sorts of things with information, creating innumerable texts and performing myriad operations with them. The internet has revolutionised this field, providing instant links between people and access to any text. Despite these achievements, there is still only an extremely weak demand for the information each of us creates. Nobody has ever really known what to do with the opinion of the ordinary private individual, and this despite the fact that every homo sapiens possesses a sliver of valuable knowledge which he is constantly accumulating and updating. He remembers and interprets what he has seen, heard and experienced, and formulates an attitude towards it. In this way each person is ceaselessly creating information, but inexcusably little effort is made to use this resource for the common good. It is as neglected as the energy of the wind or of waterfalls. Let's face it, there are many situations where it would do no harm to know what rank-and-file citizens think, or know, or believe to be fair, rather than taking account only of the views of the top echelons of society. We see the main advantage of a market economy as being the way it is able to use knowledge dispersed through society. Each participant in the market possesses information known only to him about his opportunities and needs. The market already stimulates the use of some of this knowledge, coordinating the actions of agents by means of prices and competition. Where it fails however, is in using laborious, outdated methods to mine extremely limited quantities of knowledge from enormous seams of information about people's lives, their judgements, intentions and assessments.

If someone is not a public figure, the lion's share of the information they create is lost without trace. We may try to salve our conscience by taking the view that this subjective, inaccurate, badly expressed, unusable information deserves nothing better. "You cannot make a silk purse out of a sow's ear," we warn, implying that 100 rank-and-file judgements are no match for one professional judgement. Sometimes, however, there can be strength in numbers and ubiquity, sometimes in speed of reaction (as when events are reported instantly by eyewitnesses in a way no newspaper can hope to match), and the information is presented in accessible, folksy language, liberated and unblinkered. We can be sure that there is a substantial benefit waiting if society can only mobilise the resources tucked away in each one of us. In this book collaborative filtering is shown to be inscribed on the banner of the New Economy because it is key to resolving this task. It appears to be an unparalleled technology for extracting a valuable product from the husk of what ordinary people have to say. It finds value in raw material which has been neglected because nobody knew how to use it. The resulting information product is far more useful than anything we currently have in the form of ratings, charts, and other summaries. In the course of the statistical averaging out to reduce these vernacular voices to overall ratings, all that is personal vanishes into a common grave. Crucial information is irrevocably lost and we are not upset in the slightest because of our ignorance. Collaborative filtering enables us to identify and satisfy a demand for subjective information. The source of the information, obviously, is individuals, but for some reason up till now nobody has thought how to process or make use of the data. The moment the use of subjective information is recognised, there will be an incentive to collect it, structure it and exploit it.

Let us take as our point of departure the shortcomings typical of current ways of processing personal judgements or consumer reactions. We don't, for example, know whose opinion ratings reflect. An average rating is useful for a producer or the mass consumer, but it is a very approximate guide for anyone whose tastes deviate from some standard statistical mean. For them a rating will invariably be too high or too low in relation to their own quirky opinion on whatever is the matter in hand. Take the UK's weekly "Top Twenty" pop songs. It is entirely probable that you will not find a single song there which speaks to you. This is typical of any chart based on statistics of sales to anyone from conservative professors to iPod addicts (with a natural bias in favour of the latter). In order to personalise the rating we need a method of filtering the judgements of people who differ from each other. We need the ability to identify who is similar and deliver to them personally the opinions of people who think the way they do. It might be, for example, that out of a million cinemagoers a movie has been seen through our eyes by only 500 people. What that 0.05% of the audience thought is what we are most likely to be interested in.

The most important aspect of the collaborative mechanism is its ability to identify groups of like-minded people. At the heart of the software's algorithm is the hypothesis that coincidence in the present can be predicted from coincidence in the past. Unlike anything done previously, grouping takes place not through psychological tests or socio-demographic data (although these may contribute), but on the basis of a directly expressed attitude to particular consumed objects, events or texts.

If two people have read a certain number of the same books (watched the same movies, listened to the same songs) and have rated them similarly, then in certain respects their views are close. This should make it useful for them to exchange opinions about items with which one is already familiar and the other not. Such is the (un)complicated heuristics on which the collaborative method is based. In order to obtain recommendations, a person must first rate a number of items (several dozen, or preferably several hundred) to create his preference profile or "taste pattern." The system compares the profiles of different people and identifies those who are similar. The logic of collaborative filtering is simple, but in practice highly complex algorithms are used in this computation. There are different approaches even to something as fundamental as defining measures of proximity. In a group of like thinkers there will be those who have seen, read, or experienced something as yet unfamiliar to their "taste neighbours." On the basis of the ratings given by the former a prediction is computed for the latter. On another occasion recipients and donors of information may change places. If opinions are processed on many items and areas of consumption – literature, cinema, music, brands and other sectors, including fringe cultural and totally utilitarian items (which it is almost impossible to find nowadays in consumer markets), one can reliably identify common ground between people and use it to compute predictions and personal recommendations. For practical purposes it is essential: (1) to collect a large number of ratings from a large number of people; (2) to form a reference group for each of them consisting of people with proximate opinions/ratings; (3) to synthesise the predictions; (4) to make the result known, on request, to the taste neighbours individually. All this is currently being done on recommendation sites constructed on the basis of collaborative filtering.

As is often the case, it is more difficult to formulate a problem than to solve it. As soon as the potential demand for subjective information is recognised, we may consider the job half done. While everything after that is no small matter, it is only technology. Recognising how to deal with subjective experience is a fundamental discovery, more far-reaching than the actual invention and elaboration of the collaborative technology which enables us to mobilise the information resources tucked away inside us.

The consumers of subjective information are essentially the same group members who are the main players in the New Economy. Somebody's personal opinion is of interest to those whose tastes, outlook and interests are close to theirs. If a person discovers something of value, it makes sense for him to bring it to the notice of like-thinkers and then, when the time comes, they will share their discoveries with him. The issue of the objective quality of information (commonly understood to be its accuracy, originality and completeness) becomes less important. Information may be objective but not hot, uninteresting, incomprehensible, superfluous and, as a result, unwanted. In the resolving of a whole range of problems, subjective criteria prove far more important, linked to tastes, interests, and background. The need is to identify groups of like-minded people on an industrial scale and enable them to exchange subjectively significant information derived from consumer experience. Only 10 years or so ago it seemed doubtful whether the processing power of computers could be up to conducting such highly intensive calculations, but today that is not an issue.

Collaborative filtering comes under the broader category of "crowdsourcing," a term introduced by *Wired* which covers the exploitation of collective intelligence and the work of volunteers for various useful purposes, including commercial purposes. Crowdsourcing is used for identifying criminals, deciphering voice recordings, and translating texts. The company TxtEagle, for example, engaged activists in Kenya to translate the instructions for Nokia telephones from English into approximately 60 local languages. Another first which made the news was the online translation of the seventh volume of Harry Potter which Chinese, Brazilian and Russian volunteers undertook for their readers.

A crowd can be mobilised to resolve not only technical but even creative tasks. Here reliance is on brainstorming to produce a far greater diversity of approaches than is likely when making conventional use of permanent staff. Procter and Gamble, for example, advertises on its website the problems it wants solved and invites an army of 100,000 volunteers to rack their brains. The successful are rewarded financially. Other well known forms of crowdsourcing are programming projects with open source code like Linux, MySQL, or the Firefox browser. The same principle is exploited in Wikipedia. Internet surfers may find themselves participating in crowdsourcing projects without intending or wishing to do so. When visiting sites each of us is supporting the work of search algorithms. These voluntary or involuntary groupings working for the common good have been around for some time. With the enhancement of communications, however, their importance increases vastly. For crowdsourcing an organiser is required to formulate the task and recruit people to work on it. An information system is needed to enable those undertaking the task to select their small part and present the results, and subsequently to enable each user to enjoy the fruits of the work they have jointly performed. Sceptics argue that this is "anthill technology," incapable of major achievements. They claim it has a low ceiling, and in that there is a grain of truth. James Surowiecki in *Wisdom of the Crowds* gives examples of how crowds fail to cope with tasks or reach erroneous conclusions. For all that, he considers them capable of many things. Clearly, you cannot be 100% sure you can create a wise crowd to order. Nevertheless, rather than rubbish the concept, it is worth trying to nudge professionals in the direction of setting tasks which will allow the crowd to show its strengths, and also of coordinating efforts and selecting ideas.

Sometimes crowdsourcing is defined very inclusively, and then much can be brought under the heading, even the working out of norms of socially acceptable behaviour or the status system. Collaborative filtering too can be seen as an example of crowdsourcing, since on Web 2.0 and Web 3.0 sites content is created by users themselves and dispersed, non-specialised labour resources are being put to use. The armoury of the Third Web, which is a combination of user-generated and user-certified content, is something to which business firms turn, mainly at present to decide which particular products they should concentrate on. For example, Threadless, a Chicago company manufacturing T-shirts, reduced the design process to an online competition in which enthusiasts provided the creative input and themselves voted on which designs were best. These were then put into production. The designers receive premiums and prizes, but most important is the opportunity of seeing their work being worn by the public. This technique is considered a pioneering example of crowdsourcing. The Japanese company Muji designs furniture in a similar manner, but with the refinement that ideas captured over the internet are further worked on by professional designers.

It is entirely justifiable to see collaborative filtering as a variety of crowdsourcing, although its scope and importance are greater, because crowdsourcing is primarily applied to specific problems, whereas consumer rating of quality is a universal approach to exploiting the web community's information resources. Collaborative filtering is hi-tech and, crucially, requires neither moderating nor manual finishing, which is one of the drawbacks of crowdsourcing. The collaborative mechanism makes it possible to derive maximum value from the crowd's ability to gather and process information. In doing so, people are engaged in areas where they have strength and are enjoying themselves, explaining their own ratings and opinions. They are both the creators and end users of an information product.

We have here a new way of exchanging information. Oddly enough, with the exception of anthropologists studying primitive societies, nobody asks why people exchange information at all. Perhaps it just seems too obvious. Socialising is so natural that there seems no need to seek a motivation for it. Yury Lotman's school of semiotics, founded in Tartu, Estonia in the 1960s, did not address this topic either. In fact, the motivation of contemporary interpersonal communication is of fundamental importance. It is a mistake to neglect it. We have only to replace the question "Why?" with "What for?" for a whole new branch of economics to grow out of the answer: Symbolic Exchange Economics. In the course of communication, resources are expended and various outcomes are possible. People communicate because they benefit from communicating. It is pleasant and/or useful, now or in the future. Whether that aim is achieved, however, and to what extent, is contingent on many factors. With whom are they communicating, about what, in what way, at what time? All of these are considerations which can be optimised. Socialising makes its possible to improve the quality of personal time and hence the quality of life. As we will see below, the concept of quality personal time is fundamental to the New Economy.

The points users award to objects in a collaborative system are in reality a rating of their personal subjective time, even if what they seem to be characterising is objects of consumption. The rating of objects by a consumer characterises the person making the rating no less than the object rated. If someone awards a rating of "excellent" to a movie, that signifies that he had a great time watching it. The database of ratings accumulating in a collaborative system is accordingly of value, apart from anything else, as a file of reports by a large number of people about the quality of their subjective time.

The idea of identifying unrecognised groups of like-minded individuals is nothing new and underlies many phenomena in life, as anybody becoming familiar with the collaborative principle will begin to see very clearly. Before a workable technology could be created on that basis, however, it was necessary to find an appropriate method of surveying people. An approach to digitising mental operations had also to be devised. When a way was found of harvesting subjective ratings numerically, it became possible to computerise the process. The first approach to working collectively with information was introduced by the Xerox Corporation in 1992, where the practical task was to enable researchers to share information about salient books, articles or papers which any member of the group came upon. A few years later the idea was developed and provided the basis for recommendation services, of which the best-known today are Netflicks (for the cinema) and Last.FM (for music). In Russia such sites are consolidated in Imhonet. Unlike the two Western resources which specialise in just one type of content, Imhonet issues recommendations in more than 20 fields, from literature to mobile telephones. Examples of how this portal works are used in the present book.

At first sight it might appear that collaborative filtering is an ingenious but limited technological toy. In fact, however, it is not just a handy technique but a fundamental principle for working with information, and it subsumes a great deal that is new and useful. We know of examples in history when some mixture of Bertholet's salt redrew the map of the world, although this occurred not when it was first observed that it could explode but when a military application for the discovery was recognised. In early Christianity the appearance of the first hermits was seen initially as merely a form of lunacy, rather than as the beginning of monasteries on which the Church, and with it European civilisation, would come to rely. Collaborative filtering is a new way of forming groups, communication clubs, like-minded communities which in the era of the New Economy will become the building blocks of society. It is thanks to collaborative filtering that, for the first time in history, we understand what to do with the opinion of a single individual. A subjective statement is transformed into a product of value to members of a group which emerges simultaneously on the basis of such statements.

2.5 Evolution of the Second Invisible Hand

One of the great achievements of economic thought was discovering the principle of the "invisible hand" of the market. Using this metaphor, Adam Smith explained how markets, and with them vast areas of human activity, are regulated without any direct exchange of information between people, through prices and the balance of supply and demand. The way this operates is that the consumer sees different prices and chooses what is best and cheapest; the producer also sees prices and decides whether he can produce goods at a profit and what volume of them he will be able to sell. Competition favours the best at the cheapest price and society reaps the benefit. If too many goods are manufactured, demand slackens, the price falls, and production is scaled back. If there is a shortage, the price rises and production is increased until supply and demand are once more in balance. Nobody needs to arbitrarily command and control how much of what is produced. The invisible hand operates through the information system of prices, which activates market forces. Perhaps, since the main factor here is observing goods and prices, we might do better to talk of invisible eyes and ears rather than a hand. Until very recently nobody considered the possibility of any other kind of coordination, and that was entirely understandable because any direct exchange of information between people which extended beyond their immediate circle would have been freighted with prohibitively high costs.

The crucial change brought about by the information technology industry, electronic mail and search engines is that communication has become a great deal cheaper. Opportunities have appeared for the person-to-person exchange of information without any middlemen, and also for public exchange of information within the community where a comment can be transmitted not "in series" to one person after another but instantly, "in parallel," to every online member of society. Since this direct exchange of information has taken off, to the famous invisible hand we can add a parallel mechanism which operates on observation not of prices but of who is buying what, for what reason, and to what effect.

This is a "second invisible hand." It has in fact always existed, but has operated even more invisibly than the first, and outside the purview of economists. It is the system of status distinctions which has ruled the world since ancient times and which functions through observation of product diversity and the rate at which products are renewed, which is how the status and membership of a particular stratum of society is made public. We have seen that this is needed in order to provide oneself with the necessary contacts and access to the circles necessary for arranging one's personal and public life. The interests which the second invisible hand coordinates are not material but are to do with relationships and communication. They affect the business sphere and the personal sphere. Accordingly, this invisible hand operates in both the economic and the symbolic field but, unlike the first hand, concerns the relationship not between goods and prices but between objects and individuals. Actions are prompted, not by standard-setting products and their prices, but by iconic personalities who are role models in one's immediate or a more remote environment. We strive to catch up with or to excel them in our own milieu, to be seen as equal or even superior to them.

The rules for climbing the symbolic social ladder are more complex than those for the financially based ladder. Product diversity is the means by which the second invisible hand orders this hierarchy and its groups, but these are based not only on property but also on categories of symbolic capital and taste. People choose items in accordance with their taste and what they can afford, and the signals their possessions transmit enable them to join in or distance themselves, and to compete with other people. They see some who are beneath them, others they consider their equals, and those to whose level they aspire. These higher and lower levels exist in parallel within the twin coordinates of money and culture. The money people have is rarely visible as such. It reveals itself only through objects. How well off a person is, is usually judged mainly by his visible possessions, but these tell us about more than wealth. They simultaneously denote taste, mentality, social status and other attributes. If the first hand regulates through the availability of goods and services, the second holds sway over groups and relationships, but its invisible operation is made visible by those same goods. The first hand operates through producers reacting to demand, while the second acts through consumers who demand particular goods they need for denoting their differences.

In the sphere in which the second hand is acting, competition is regulated not by price but by more complex, compound signals. In every age society, as it searches for orderliness, needs to be able to produce a seam of differences between individuals which it can present and detect, a process which develops in accordance with the laws of information economics. Whether to make contact with a person or not is a decision always taken within certain time constraints. No matter how desperately you may need information about a potential acquaintance, you have to make do with what you can gather in the time available. Given unlimited time you could, if you so wished, find out pretty much everything about the person you are interested in, but is it worth it? As Herbert Simon, one of the fathers of information economics, put it, a search continues until its costs outweigh its anticipated benefits. In accordance with the saying, "the best is the enemy of the good," a person stops when he reaches what is acceptable.

Consumer society provides a signalling system and practices which enable people either to draw closer or to distance themselves. The effectiveness of the system depends on its speed, how much work it involves, and how complete the mutual "transparency" is which it provides. This affects the quality of the environment in which people live, the quality of their communications, and ultimately the quality of their life.

While a section of society is busy creating and deciphering ever more ingenious codes of stratification, the gatecrashers are not idle. There is a kind of arms race which ensures that, if a visible or invisible club becomes overfull after invasion by unwelcome visitors, the core members will refurbish its entry codes in order to return their ability to recognise each other and partition off a new club accessible only to their elite. This is most evident in fashion, where innovations are introduced rapidly in order to make sure that the non-elite majority cannot keep up. The system of ciphers accordingly becomes more complex at an accelerating rate. Thanks to the internet and its blogosphere, extremely private aspects of the personality are exposed to public view. Communication has evolved from the crude Veblen signals to a subtle system of visual imagery and is well on the way to the next stage – unpacking the interior baggage of individuals. Here there await us the most interesting secrets: preferences, educational background, interests and enthusiasms, and attitudes to all sorts of events. Little of this can be readily imitated by spending money.

In considering the internet as a catalyst for the operating of the second invisible hand, let us not forget that ultra-high-speed correspondence is not by any means all we need for effective communication. The fact that sending messages has become easier has brought about not a decrease but an increase in the costs of shovelling through piles of emails. Ever speedier communication does not necessarily make rational choice less onerous. The benefits of being able to obtain information more easily can be nullified by the increase in its quantity and the number of attempts needed, and at this point limitations make themselves felt which fall into the province of attention economics. The solution needs to be sought in automating the sorting of texts in accordance with personal requirements.

2.6 The Economic Sense of Collaborative Filtering: Division of Labour in the Testing of Experience Goods

The world of the New Economy has an abundance of goods whose consumer qualities are difficult to assess in advance from the manufacturer's specifications. These are so-called experience goods, which have to be tried out. There is also a category of search goods which can be chosen from their description, but these too have almost entirely migrated into the camp of experience goods. A television might at first sight appear to be a search good, since you can check its specifications before buying it, but there may be several dozen of these parameters, making it difficult to summarise their value. Moreover, such important constituents of value as design, brand and price are not categorised as functional, utilitarian values. It is simpler just to try them out. This goes for many, if not most, present-day goods, which is perfectly natural in view of the diversity of models released on to the market. A car might seem the classic example of a search good, but these too are becoming an experience good. You climb into your new luxury off-roader only to find the suspension unacceptably hard. You cannot tell how smooth the ride is going to be from a brochure. That is why you need a test drive. In a whole range of cases, however, that kind of pre-purchase sampling is impossible because it would be tantamount to full consumption. Having experienced it, there would be no reason to buy.

The dilemma is that everything has to be experienced before you can tell whether the goods are suitable or not, and it is impossible to test everything. The solution is to seek the recommendations of people you trust and who have already experienced the wares you are interested in. People giving advice to each other is as old as the hills, but collaborative filtering brings a fundamentally new quality to collective processing of information. Each person tries something out and, with the aid of collaborative algorithms, their individual experience goes into the collective money bank and frees many other people from needless testing and errors. This principle of division of the labour of testing is analogous to the way groups of geologists operate, dividing up a location into plots and subsequently sharing information in order not to duplicate work.

As an example, let us consider what this approach can do for the cultural industries. It is generally accepted that they suffer from a disproportion between the conveyor belt, production of output and the "manual" testing of quality by professional critics, who are drowning in floods of content and obliged to work beyond their credible capacity. Because they are overloaded, the quality-control filters become clogged, as can be seen if one takes a look at the movies most recently awarded Oscars. The reader or cinemagoer who tries to dispense with them is deluged with great quantities of unsorted trash. In order somehow to keep up with the increasing volume of output, experts proliferate beyond all reason, with the result that it is high time to give ratings to the critics themselves. There are hundreds of movie festivals, and an order of magnitude more literary prizes, with the result that they attract little attention and convey nothing useful to any significant number of people.

Collaborative technology makes it possible to mobilise an army of volunteers and restore the balance. No matter how fast content is generated, it is countered by a no less massive system of selection by the crowd. A galaxy of goods is balanced by myriad centres of critical evaluation. Commercial producers can spew on to the market as much third-rate rubbish as they like, disguising it with alluring covers, but the consumer community will unerringly reject all that is substandard. Unsaleable goods will be sent off to be pulped or shredded. Such is the collaborative antidote to adverse selection in culture.

As has been mentioned, collaborative filtering makes it possible not to average information out, not to melt it down in the furnace of general opinion, but to deliver it personally to individuals to whom it is going to be of interest. This is similar to how a fractionating column works in the petrochemical industry: at each level, in our case at the corresponding point on the scale of taste, the fraction of opinion is extracted which is appropriate for a particular user. It is possible to figure out a monetary equivalent for this added information in terms of increased efficiency in the consumption of culture by people who have made use of recommendations.

2.7 New Technologies, New Institutions

Like any major innovation, collaborative filtering brings many possible applications in its wake. New institutions and sub-institutions sprout up, new rules for life and living in society.

We have mentioned its use as an antidote to adverse selection. Collaborative filtering makes it possible to restore parity of knowledge between the consumer and producer in respect of the quality of goods, blocking the tendency to adverse selection which invariably appears where there is asymmetry of information.

In addition to the new institution of collective critical assessment by consumers, for the first time in history we have a full-blown system of feedback between the consumer and producer. In the past, markets contented themselves with feedback derived from sales statistics, but box-office takings tells us only how much people have paid, not how satisfied they were. The post-experience assessment of a product may differ markedly from what it was before the purchase. This is particularly applicable to goods infrequently consumed, or consumed only once, which today is the dominant pattern. With collaborative filtering, signals about quality are received from people who have already experienced the good and are not merely judging it from hearsay. Moreover, we are dealing now with the direct expression of consumers' views rather than some interpretation of their behaviour, like the number of clicks on an internet page displaying goods. (This is the information currently used in order not to annoy customers with endless surveys.) Never before has a producer been able to discover what a purchaser thinks about his goods as clearly and rapidly as he can on a recommendation site. Importantly, the customers themselves do not know each other's ratings. This provides a handicap for heavily advertised goods like movies, where the pioneer consumers are passively followed by all the others, taking their cue not from the impression the movie made (which is unknown), but from the mere fact that tickets were purchased. The phenomenon is known as a "non-informative information cascade" or, to put it more bluntly, following the herd.

Managing anything without feedback brings you up against almost insuperable difficulties. When feedback becomes available, it enables a fundamentally different approach in the social (non-commercial) sector, and in particular to cultural policy.

Let us, however, not run ahead of ourselves but move now to practical institutions and applications which flow directly from collaborative filtering and which have either been approved or are in the pipeline for the very near future.

2.7.1 Web 3.0

One such institution, which is already functioning, is the so-called Third Web. I put in that "so-called" because until recently something quite different was understood by the term, namely the "semantic web." The need for the semantic web made itself felt in connection with the extreme "noisiness" of the internet. It became necessary to find a method of automatically detecting the type and quality of texts, in order to save time when trying to select the best and most relevant of them. Many hopes are pinned on the semantic web, which is a computerised linguistic analysis of file content.

In my view, it is easier to open the treasure chest with a different key, namely collaborative filtering, where quality is being analysed by the users themselves. Although their opinions (ratings) are shamelessly subjective, they are addressed to people for whom their value is their subjectivity. Subjective certification of quality is appropriate when addressed to subjective perceptions of quality.

Web 3.0, which is user generation and filtering of texts, is in my belief the way forward for the internet. In the previous phase, texts on the net were sought using search engines, but now the era has arrived of personalised, individual delivery of content. As a result, every user will be able to receive what is of interest to him personally. Web 3.0 is a kind of search engine which, in response to a user's search, provides a personalised selection of content. Web 3.0 is the next stage in evolution of the internet after Web 2.0.

Web 2.0 is user-generated texts and images. People keep personal diaries in which they write whatever they like, or present texts, photos, videos, or pass on other people's materials which they have liked. This is all laid out in minimally classified portions, with no ranking in terms of quality. It is not difficult to understand why Web 2.0 was a winner with creators of websites: it was a means of obtaining free content. People are reluctant to pay on the internet, but servers and other infrastructure need to be funded. If you have also to pay for creating content, supporting a site becomes expensive. Professional editing is an appreciable budget item. Accordingly, creators of websites moved to foraging, farming out the creation of content to users. In return the users receive a forum for socialising and expressing themselves. This would be fine, except that people can only write and photograph to the best of their ability, and one ends up literally scavenging a crumb at a time in the search for interesting content among all the amateur offerings and repetitive quotation. This is time-consuming and appreciably detracts from the satisfactoriness of the pastime. Web 2.0 is users' Do-It-Yourself in terms of content, with all the advantages and disadvantages associated with it.

Web 3.0 differs from Web 2.0 in that users not only search for or create content, but filter it themselves. From the viewpoint of the end user, it will not matter who generates or hosts content, users or professionals. It all grows out of the highly diverse spawning ground of culture: hundreds of thousands of songs a year, 250 decent movies, ten times as many purely commercial movies, millions of written texts, video blogs and postings. All this huge quantity of stuff will be certified and individually packaged by the community of a collaborative site as fractions in the column of taste.

Sorting by quality is important for content (and indeed all material output) of any kind. There is one sector, however, where the task is particularly urgent, and that is in the filtering of topical content. News, articles, essays, current analysis, interesting video and photos, blog entries, jokes etc. all have a short shelf-life, and more than any other content need to be packaged and delivered to their target audience rapidly. You will sooner or later hear about the movie which won the Cannes Film Festival and will have little difficulty seeing it any time. There are, of course, very good but little known movies which get shown at second or third rank festivals but which almost never go on general release. A recommendation service will help them to emerge from the shadows, but here too there is no great urgency. The situation is quite different for content which dates rapidly. This is where user filtering is particularly valuable, and the service supporting it is essential.

On such a collaborative filtering site people can post anything that has grabbed them: news, jokes, analysis, their own biography, cartoons etc., and the collaborative programme packages all this and issues it in accordance with users' preferences. Each participant receives a personalised selection containing all the things which people in his reference group (people whom the system has identified as taste neighbours, plus anyone the user has asked should be added to his list) have rated highly. The technology frees you from scouring the net and provides a selection of content which merits your attention. It is also suitable for packaging the periodical press, enabling readers with a single mouse click to receive a collection of the most relevant articles published in one or two dozen publications. Each person probably browses one, or at most two or three publications, which means that interesting articles will almost inevitably have been overlooked.

Some readers of the mass media may belong to the same group as a particular user and for them it is no big deal to flag up interesting articles which, thanks to collaborative filtering, then become a shared asset of the group. On the f1000biology.com website, for example, leading scientists annotate publications they consider deserving of attention. By doing so, by performing wholly routine actions and nothing extra, people jointly work up a pool of the best information materials for their joint use. It may well transpire that the most interesting communications do not arrive from sources readers have been accustomed to use. Web 3.0 technology thus makes it possible to raise one's game, working far more efficiently with media materials and specialist literature.

2.7.2 *Smart Introductions, Meaningful Messages*

Another innovation associated with collaborative filtering technology is advanced internet introductions. In itself this facility might not have a right to the grand title of an institution but for the enormous role which encounters and contacts play in human lives. On the internet, introduction services are ultra-popular, although it seems quite difficult to find friends through them and, judging by end results, time spent there is mostly time wasted. The process of searching, browsing through photographs, presenting yourself, flirting by email or chat, all goes according to the book until the moment of meeting in reality. People have rushed to make friends online, realising that the barriers which hinder intimacy are lowered there. Online undoubtedly does win out in terms of convenience and delicacy at the phase of coquettishness and checking each other out, but the advantages evaporate when you go off-line. Selection is through photographs and socio-demographics. People naturally try to show themselves in the best light, and allowance is made for this, but nevertheless the virtual and real images tend to be so different that most often the introduction leads nowhere, if we ignore one-off sexual encounters. The latter keep sites of this nature afloat. For so-called dating the service as it exists today would be fine if it had not been turned into a marketing medium for (semi-) professional services of an intimate nature.

Quite apart from online flirtation, which survives on the fantasies and boredom of some users and the sexual voracity of others, there is a need for friendships of a different kind. This includes the search for lifelong companions, and also the wish just to make the acquaintance of interesting new people. Such meetings of minds are, however, for the time being still arranged mainly in the old way, off-line. Shared journeys, entertainment, sport, education, the wish to discuss issues that matter to you with another person – for all this recommender technology might have been specially invented.

An example of the practical implementation of this idea is the Russian-language service "Smart Introductions" on the internet at http://imhonet.ru/users/dating/, where three filters are used to select potentially interesting people. The first is the standard socio-demographic one: sex, age, place of study and residence, marital situation, photograph, etc. This functionality is found nowadays on every profile site. The second filter, by shared interests, is also widely applied (for example on the "In Touch"/*Vkontakte* site) and will be helpful if someone is looking for tennis partners, fellow amateur photographers or karaoke enthusiasts. Finally, the third, collaborative, filter is entirely without analogy. People can use it to find partners for themselves whose tastes are close to theirs, not only in terms of culture but in any sphere where taste preferences play a role. It is one thing to be a fitness fanatic or to enjoy playing table football, but quite another to share that enthusiasm with people with whom you have a lot to talk about. All three filters function automatically with just a few clicks.

The choosing of like-minded people or taste neighbours is an essential but intermediate phase in collaborative filtering. On the Imhonet.ru site it has been turned into a freestanding end product. The programme recommends interesting people to users in just the same way it recommends works of art. As a bonus, there is nothing to stop you from taking a closer look at the person the system has selected. The automatic selection greatly reduces the number of "possibles," after which it is time to resort to manual filtering. You can look through the full list of a person's interests, the books he reads, the movies, brands, and wines he likes. If he looks promising you can read his blog, reviews and comments. Any friendship, platonic or romantic, is going to benefit from the opportunity to select in accordance with tastes and interests. Having found candidates for friendship from their photographs, the next step, for example, could be to filter for those who like Fyodor Tyutchev's poetry.

2.8 The Gratuity Economy: Retrospective Payment and Group Motivation

Such tools as Web 3.0 and Smart Introductions give an idea of the basic potential of applied collaborative technology. In both cases all that is required is the recommender service itself, but one other far-reaching innovation is arriving which fits very logically with collaborative filtering. This is a move to voluntary post factum payment. These two principles taken together provide the conditions for the appearance of a whole family of social institutions, all of them with links on the one hand to the group economy, and on the other to the gratuity economy. The gratuity economy involves economic exchanges which are unconventional in that goods and services are delivered without money but in the expectation that they will be paid for after being used. Moreover, the recompense is voluntary, that is, it is left entirely to the good judgement of the consumer. Such a radical departure from the traditional scheme of paying upfront will, no doubt, seem rather startling. Absurd, however, it is not, if we take cognisance of just how uncertain product quality has become. There is indeed a further question to be answered: are the goods even necessary or could one get by perfectly well without them?

There is a further argument in favour of post-factum payments. Bearing in mind the plentiful supply of practically everything, including producers, and the shrinking numbers of consumers, it is becoming unclear who should pay whom. Should listeners pay the songwriter for the days he has spent on his composition, or, on the contrary, should the songwriter pay the listeners for having motivated him to enjoy those days of inspiration and for having listened to the result? Symbolic communications are different in being reciprocal, mutually motivated, with equal input from the two sides. That is why it is so difficult to fit them into the framework of remunerative, impersonal, utilitarian contracts. A gratuity payment system is the future of the New Economy, the reverse of what is customary.

There is a further reason for moving to post-factum payments. In a number of areas the traditional mechanism of competition is failing. A typical example is the digital cultural industries where Adam Smith's invisible hand of the market has nothing to guide it, whether in terms of price or quantities of production. The content files all cost the same, and it is difficult to keep copying of them under control. Areas where there is no natural scarcity, which means the greater part of symbolic production, can only be fitted into the framework of conventional economics with the use of considerable force. This, specifically, is the role of copyright, which we will discuss below. With the development of digital technologies, some markets have arisen which, in certain respects, are soundly rooted in the conventional economy. In other respects, however, they hover weightlessly in realms where laws premised on a limited supply of goods simply do not apply. It is far from clear how a business should be run when its goods are effectively being circulated free. If people so wish, they can obtain them without having to pay for them. The natural reflex of the system is to pretend that nothing much has happened and to carry on following the old routine. With time, however, it becomes evident that forcible restraint not only demands constant pressure, but is also accompanied by negative effects (like any attempt to unite things which are incompatible).

Where the economic and the symbolic lack any genetic kinship, which primarily means in the area of scarcity, they stubbornly repel each other. Seeing the determination with which the state rushes to the defence of copyright, you recognise that it is, at least to some extent, trying to maintain the status quo in order to give the cultural industries time to adapt to the new realities. At the same time, supporting the monopoly on culture of a number of major corporations unquestionably detracts from market efficiency.

If the economic nature of the product has radically changed, does it make sense to persist with the traditional scheme of exchange? If for objective reasons it is difficult to restrict and sell goods, may the solution not be to offer them on the basis of voluntary recompense? That is, to move systematically to post-factum payment or post-exchange recompense based on trust. In the abstract, the move is obvious, but of little value if no mechanism is proposed or conditions created to ensure that masses of people will indeed pay and that the revenues so collected will be sufficient to motivate conscientious producers. If such a mechanism can be created, we need have no further worries for the future of the gratuity economy.

The basic idea behind the new scheme is that people first consume a product, and then pay for it if they so choose. What producer is going to agree to take such a risk, to violate the accepted principle of getting paid upfront? This is something which until now has been attempted only as part of an advertising promotion. In actual fact, however, the approach of post-factum payment only appears paradoxical and utopian. In the right conditions and with a change of attitude it can become the norm. Like so much in human behaviour, the way we use money is a matter of habit and beliefs formed as the result of lessons taught by life. The practice of paying for a book but being given a load of trash is no less paradoxical, but people accept it. This kettle of fish suits the producer well, especially a producer with no interest in quality, but if we take the side of the consumer, should we not allow him to ascertain the quality of the product first and only then to settle up? The trader holds back, fearing that this will merely result in his being paid nothing and he will go bankrupt. Collaborative filtering, however, is firmly anchored in group behaviour and the long-term benefits of collaboration. That is why it is an ideal trampoline for the introduction of post-factum payment. What most militates against the post-factum scheme is an anxiety that a person will pretend not to have liked something which he did in fact enjoy, and that he will use that pretext not to pay. In other words, he will behave like a typical freeloader (who does not pay for a good and exploits its accessibility at the same time as others have paid up). The trick is that the member of a group will find it to his disadvantage to play false, because this is likely to cost him more in the end. By not conscientiously paying, a consumer, whether he likes it or not, gives a product a low rating when he should have given it a high rating. To that extent, he distorts his preference profile and is ejected automatically from his group of like-minded people, losing group privileges and in particular the right to enjoy recommendations. He would do well to think twice before being greedy.

Will group sanctions be enough to deter, for example, somebody who has dined in a restaurant from leaving without paying? Restaurateurs have experimented with post-factum payment for meals. They were taking a risk, of course, but there has never been a case of their being left out of pocket. If we are not talking about a one-off tourist trap but a place where you are known, then to leave without paying is to lose face. Unflattering rumours will circulate and next time you will find yourself barred. There have been about a dozen experiments with post-factum payment.

A recent one involved the Radiohead alternative rock group. One of their albums was distributed on a post-payment basis and grossed many millions. Despite the pioneering nature of such actions, we should not pin excessive hopes on them. Are they perhaps successful only because they are exceptional, because they are so rare and extravagant? It need not follow that all will go equally smoothly when such actions become commonplace and lose their aura of exoticism. For a gratuity scheme to become the norm something more, something systemic, something binding, is needed to encourage payers and impose sanctions on freeloaders.

No doubt it is sensible to test the method with small stakes in order not to lead people into temptation before the habit is established. This is typically the situation with digital goods, which rarely involve large sums of money. It seems significant that the retrospective payment scheme originated on the internet, where software is distributed free in anticipation of later gratuity payment.

Take the trade in digitised books. Text files cost nothing to print and distribute, so it is less risky to supply them on a post-payment basis than, for example, steak and chips. If people choose to do so, they will pay, but if they don't little is lost. Previous experience has shown that it is advisable for a producer to name a recommended sum to establish a norm, and then invite the consumer to express his rating against that: the greater the satisfaction, the higher the payment. If on one occasion a group member pays more and on another pays nothing, these facts are visible to the system and will automatically be reflected in his profile and from there on his position in the group. This will prevent anyone from being able to use group recommendations without paying honestly.

The problem of the freeloader is an age-old problem in the creating of social goods. The producer is demotivated when people exploit the fruits of his labour for nothing. By tying the post-factum payment scheme in with collaborative processing of information we are using a standard method to overcome the curse of social goods by transforming them into "club" goods. In a club you are a long-term member, you are on view, and your reputation matters. If somebody comes day in day out to the same place with the same people and they notice that time and again he fails to pay, there will be sanctions. What if the members of the club are his colleagues? In such a situation, petty swindling will prove even more unprofitable. Where everybody knows everybody else's face, a freeloader is not going to last long. The other members will either re-educate him or chuck him out.

One other factor which sustains micro-patronage is that people customarily respond to good with good and do not needlessly burden their soul with the sin of ingratitude. This is confirmed by the ancient ritual of *kule*, the exchange of ritual gifts, which is widespread among preliterate peoples. To accept something as a gift and not respond with a gift is tantamount to allowing yourself to be possessed by the *hau*, an alien spirit. It generates bad vibrations. Reciprocating gifts is an accepted principle, and if in addition to that there is a visible or invisible club to which people belong, and disregarding this norm will result in sanctions, then it is downright foolhardy not to behave properly. This is why people pay five times the price for designer goods, although they know that non-brand (although possibly licensed) fashions are virtually indistinguishable. It is odd that supporting high-end brands is not regarded by society as a form of patronage, when that is in effect what it is. If you try to be too smart and not pay, you risk losing something more important than the money saved, namely the quality of the relationships in which you are embedded. There are no end of reasons why it would be embarrassing to be stingy, especially if there is a norm by comparison with which you look bad. Mutually regulated behaviour underwrites the stability of many of life's norms, and this is precisely the kind of link which binds gratuity payment and collaborative (club) filtering.

Micro-patronage is admirably suited to the scheme of unmediated commerce. The user saves money by cutting out middlemen while at the same time obtaining a product which accords with his taste. These would seem ideal conditions for patronage, and is it so rare for people to express appreciation that we must imagine they will never show gratitude by paying up? People clap in the theatre without grudging the time it takes. They present bouquets, although the performers might prefer something more practical, like money. But if it is impractical for an impulsive member of the audience to slip the leading lady a tenner, who is to say that, given the opportunity to express his appreciation in monetary terms, perhaps with a couple of keystrokes, there would be any problem? The internet is highly convenient for the micro-patron but, as luck would have it, the habit has become ingrained there of not paying for anything.

Here a modification of post-factum gratuity payment might prove effective, dispensing with money and accepting a barter in time by agreeing to pay attention to advertising. This is particularly convenient on the internet, where a gratuitous impulse can be given instant expression. If the user has been pleased by a text or recommendation or other service, meaning that he has enjoyed some high-quality time, it is entirely logical for him to pay in the same currency of time by donating attention. He does not need to dig in his pocket for change or even to send a premium-rate text message, or submit to a lot of other hassle which is hardly justified in the case of a micro-payment. If he has enjoyed a certain number of minutes or hours of pleasure, he can make a proportionate payment in the form of his time. Monetising accumulated attention is no problem: that is what advertisers are there for. The post-payment scheme merged with settling up by paying attention may prove to be the long-awaited business model for net media. In the future it may be possible to extend its use to other segments of symbolic production.

At present the media oblige the consumer to watch advertisements and that is how they are funded. Television and radio slip advertisements into the flow of their video and audio content. Newspapers, magazines and websites incorporate them, sometimes tactfully, sometimes obtrusively, but essentially the model is an imperative: "Come on, look at this!" Paid television uses the opposite technique. Supposedly collecting payment for content, it is actually making the viewer pay for not having to watch the advertising to which he would be subjected on "free" channels. The model we are considering is different, in that the advertising would not be imposed and neither would you have to buy yourself out of it. It would also have been filtered, which would make it both more effective and less tedious.

The gratuity payment scheme is not something which grows naturally out of collaborative technology. It is a separate, fundamental innovation which goes to the very heart of the institution of money, but collaborative filtering is a convenient bridgehead for running the practice in and popularising an approach whose time has come. The idea of post-factum payment is in the air we breathe. With every passing month there are reports of new experiments, but the scheme will only take off if gratuity payments can fulfil several functions at once. Major institutions like money never appear for just one reason and never serve just one purpose. They always appear at the point where many interests intersect and perform many functions. Micro-patronage is no exception. It has a real prospect of becoming widely accepted only if it performs several parallel tasks: (1) signalling the quality of goods or services and providing direct feedback from the consumer to the producer; (2) enabling the consumer to make his views heard; (3) generating revenue for producers of cultural products, and royalties paid to creators and rights owners; (4) auditing the symbolic realm (which we discuss in detail in Chap. 3).

If we bring together all the arguments in favour of micro-patronage, they will undoubtedly suffice to justify implementing it on a large scale. Those already evident are:

1. The psychological value of charity for the donor himself;
2. Unmediated links between consumer and producer and the opportunity of personally making fair payment to the latter;
3. The sense of community of a group of people behaving charitably;
4. Reducing the value of money and increasing the value of time, which is a characteristic of well-functioning societies;
5. An easy way of donating.

2.8.1 *Insuring Cultural Goods*

Collaborative filtering creates the conditions necessary for insuring cultural goods. At first glance this appears to be an oxymoron. People usually insure things against damage which can be documented. That art can wound the soul there is no doubt, but can it be documented? Disappointed hopes from a movie? What criteria would underpin an insurance claim? In fact, all that is necessary is for the claimant to say it was so. The safeguard will be that same mechanism of mutual regulation and restraint which underlies the post-factum payment scheme.

Let us take cinema as an example. At present the cinemagoer is sold the right of admission to the auditorium. There is no guarantee about the quality of the movie. A recommender service can provide its user with a prediction of how much he is going to enjoy it. With a click of the mouse he can call up a whole list of movies, sort them by their predicted rating, and from then on watch only good movies. Unlike the movie maker or the movie distributor, a recommender service is answerable for the reliability of its predictions, which is its basic product. If after the viewing the user rates the movie worse than was predicted, the service has to pay out. A simple calculation suggests that up to half the cost of a ticket, 200 rubles out of 400, could be refunded to all complainants without exception. Beyond that, refunds could be made only to those who paid an insurance premium.

What will save the insurer from bankruptcy when users rush to him, claiming they did not like their recommended movies and demanding refunds? That same restraining factor of reputation within a group. It makes no sense at all for the participants of a collaborative system to attempt fraud. They risk losing more than they will gain. In order to be in a position to join an insurance scheme, a person will have had to build up his profile by rating a minimum of 100 movies and to have been on the site for a considerable period of time. Before he can lodge insurance claims he will have had to buy tickets and watched quite a few movies, since the recommender system issues high-quality predictions, rarely makes mistakes, and without tickets there will be no insurance payouts. If he does nevertheless fraudulently make an insurance claim for a movie he actually liked, the whole chain reaction will begin. His profile will be distorted, he will be ejected from the reference group, and the quality of recommendations will decline. There will no doubt be people who will not be deterred by this, but such exceptions will be covered by the insurance premiums collected from all the others.

2.8.2 A New Business Model for the Electronic Media: Customised Trust Advertising

The post-factum payment scheme is a pivotal innovation from which much else can follow. It is nice to be good, it is unprofitable to be greedy because group sanctions will follow. Such is the basic stick-and-carrot logic, but this can be taken further. Instead of merely restricting the privileges of non-payers and symbolically encouraging donors, the latter can also receive monetary rewards. The user is already prepared to pay, he is additionally under pressure from group sanctions, and here as a trump card he is going to be paid a bonus. The idea of paying a donor is suggestive of the fallacy of perpetual motion. A person pays and then gets his money back. Where do we get the grease for the machine and what has happened to energy loss through friction? In order to find the solution, let us remind ourselves of several basics of advertising theory.

An advertisement pursues three goals: (1) to provide information about goods and their producer; (2) to hook the purchaser and program his choice; (3) to evoke trust by finding a way to signal the product's quality. Strange as it may seem, trust does arise, despite the fact that the seller is praising his own goods. The paradox is described in detail in game theory. The advertisement's effectiveness comes from the already familiar sacrifice mechanism: by spending on advertising the seller is giving a pledge and demonstrating he is confident that shoddy goods will never be associated with his name and cease to be bought.

The implied message is that "Things which are advertised are good," and in most cases that is right. Not always, admittedly. By no means all goods and services are repeatedly purchased, which means that once the money has been paid it does not matter all that much whether the customer is satisfied or not. He will have no opportunity to complain. The proportion of such one-off goods in the New Economy is growing. Moreover, there may be a sufficient interval between acts of consumption for the compromised product to disappear from sale or be presented in a different guise, or the purchaser may simply forget his negative experience. In effect, these are variants of single-experience goods. In the second place, disappointing and losing a particular customer may not matter if the producer knows he can find plenty of others who will not know what happened. In the third place, part of the problem may in any case lie with the customer himself who may not know what he is doing or misuse the product. He may ultimately write off the failures as being his own fault and keep trying the goods. There are other subtleties which we need not go into. The grand solution was to introduce brands. These work like aggregators and guarantors of trust and cover a whole range of goods sold under their logo. There is a kind of joint liability here where, if one product fails to meet the customer's expectations, a shadow of suspicion will fall on the brand's entire range. Brands do therefore have a worthwhile incentive to deal with customer dissatisfaction.

Even brands have some scope for mischief but that is not the point at issue. Our concern is the kind of social costs which result from the present system where the main source of information about the quality of goods is the seller. "White box" goods, that is unbranded goods of identical quality, and sometimes even made by the same manufacturer, cost 30–40% less than branded goods. Would it not be better to listen to the voice of those who have bought goods and are prepared to judge them with greater impartiality? We come back to collaborative practice, but this time the aspect which interests us is not its ability to inform consumer choice or to mesh supply and demand, but a fundamentally new form of advertising in which the praise of goods can come from the end users. How so? After all, one's instant reaction is that advertisers will welcome the monitoring of their products by users much as they might welcome a fishbone in the gullet. Advertisers cast aspersions over personal endorsements, claiming that they are paid for and hence insincere. There is, however, a way in which these seemingly incompatible elements can be admirably reconciled.

It can happen that a user really has liked goods, and has both the motivation and the mechanism to publicise his assessment. If conventional advertising deserves to be trusted because of the element of pledging, then the variety of advertisement we are about to discuss deserves it even more.

Let us imagine that there are some really high-quality goods on the market which are having difficulty finding their ideal purchaser. They are getting lost among all the low-quality offerings. Let us also imagine that a number of people have nevertheless been fortunate enough to come across them and to appreciate their merit. For the firm producing the goods, these people are worth their weight in gold. They are a living advertisement. The problem is that what they have to say about the product is not being widely heard. Now let us suppose that the opinion of these admiring customers can be stated in public and brought individually to the attention of people it might potentially interest. Suppose further that the people who rated the goods so highly now sign a contract to advertise them. That is a brief outline of the variety of advertisement we are talking about. Let us look at it in more detail.

The first priority is honesty and trust. It is one thing to praise a product disinterestedly, but quite another to do so with an eye to potential dividends, which could lead to all manner of goods being praised to the skies. There is a difference here also for those on the receiving end. It is one thing to listen to advice given without an ulterior motive, but another if you know that the person making the recommendation is being paid to do so. Has not the crucial basis of trust already been eroded? We have seen the answer: opportunism is held in check by the already familiar mechanism of restraint and mutually regulated behaviour.

The second issue is, where is the financial reward going to come from? This brings us to the crux of the matter. The user is invited to advertise on his pages only those goods which he rates highly. In real life, off-line, people tell other people what they have liked or enjoyed. Why not online? Until now one link has been missing: a means of coordinating the demand for advice with the supply. More simply, it has not been clear who to accept recommendations from and who to address them to. Collaborative filtering solves the problem because bringing compatible people together is what it does. In order to adapt offline word-of-mouth recommendations to the internet, we need to identify objects rated highly by a user and then obtain his agreement to place an advertisement for the businesses involved. The advertisement will be spectacularly well targeted because it will be seen mainly by people who attach special weight to the opinions of that particular user, and accordingly the goods demonstrated are very likely to interest them. Rating various goods and services and selecting like-minded people are among the basic functions of a recommendation site, but why should a user agree to advertise? We have already said, he will be paid to do so.

The detailed scheme of a customised trust advertisement is as follows. The system "sees" all positively rated items and invites users to advertise goods they have genuinely liked. In order to accept the proposal the user has only to tick the items he agrees to advertise. Needless to say, these can only be objects he has already rated highly. If somebody prefers BMWs to all other cars and is proud of it, why should he not announce the fact a little more publicly than usual? Having obtained the agreement of a pool of such users, the system can compile a summary list of items which can be advertised on the site, and this can be brought to the attention of potential advertisers.

The advertiser can see how many users are willing to advertise his goods. He can see the number of hits the users' pages receive and the potential target audience of an advertisement placed there. All involved are in a position to sign a contract. Payment for the advertisement is directly linked to its effectiveness, which is a recognised advantage of the internet. This scheme also makes it possible to determine the contribution of each user and the proportion of advertising revenue due to him. The advertisement is placed on a person's home page and on those he has been involved in creating, and all viewings of these pages are added up, so there should be no problem about how to divide the revenue. Trust advertising can work not only on recommender portals, but equally on any site with collaborative filtering functionality. The main thing is availability of a valid user profile. Part of this profile can be generated on a site specialising, for example, in cigars, with the accounting carried out on the central recommender portal. In this way, alongside contextual advertising, the trust advertisement can provide a new source of income for the whole internet.

This business model may suggest an analogy with sandwich board men pacing the streets, but this would be unfair since those participating in a trust advertisement programme are not promoting anything as part of their job and are not demoted to the status of a walking advertising hoarding. Those who wear particular brands of clothing, carry bags with logos or drive cars are not likened to sandwiches. Everybody is advertising the goods they use in public, and advertising themselves through the goods they wear. Everybody is their own sandwich. At the very least, this approach is preferable to arbitrarily imposing advertisements on users' pages. And, needless to say, trust advertising should be paid at higher rates.

There are a couple of other considerations. This scheme is a fundamentally new kind of advertising. It is not the firm praising itself to the skies, or some consumer bureau which might have its own agenda. The product is being attested to by its end-user, a person with a name, a history and a reputation. We are close to the ideal where goods speak for themselves, or at least make themselves heard through the voices of those who appreciate them. Something of particular value is that the targeted recipient knows whose voice is singing the praise. In essence this is no longer pure advertising but something halfway between promotion and a system of personal advice and endorsement. It enables a real partnership to be formed between the producer and his consumers based on opportunities and needs, and a reciprocated appreciation resulting from it. It is that rare compound of goodwill, sympathy and convenience which you come across in local markets but which has disappeared from global markets because of the fracturing of human contact and the depersonalisation of the producer.

Nowadays, exchange relationships are increasingly based on the principle of who can outwit whom, something facilitated by the practice of discounts and sales. As a result, relations degenerate to an inflexible scenario, which is disappointing. It is difficult to think of an industry which has had more influence on the modern way of life than aviation, including aircraft manufacturers, airlines, and other players in the sector. The frequency of strikes and bankruptcies indicates, however, that this highly complex sector is insufficiently appreciated. Unlike designer brands, for which people have little hesitation in paying super-premium prices, people booking flights usually go to extreme measures to economise. This despite the fact that wearing a haute couture dress for a couple of hours has almost become more expensive than taking a business class flight across the Atlantic. We are not suggesting renunciation of market competition, but a warming of the micro-climate of commerce through direct human contacts would be in the interests of all conscientious players. By taking advantage of customised advertising and the concomitant trust it enjoys in groups of like-minded people, a firm will gain an incomparably better return: the internet equivalent of a good reputation.

But what if a user generates artificially high ratings in order to boost his earnings by advertising as many goods as possible? It might be interesting to try, but it would be counterproductive. The profile would be distorted, no appropriate reference group would be found, and the page would not be seen by those it was intended for. If an advertisement goes to the wrong address it produces less effect (as can be tracked on the internet) and will not be remunerative. A user who decides to try to play the system will have little success, and his reputation and goodwill will be dented. These are something the system can compute from the reactions of other users to a particular individual's actions.

For all that, some distortions and abuses are possible and even inevitable, but they will not be decisive. No matter what people are advertising, the business model will ensure that their recompense is linked to demand for the information they create. The more alluring the advertising of goods is for users, the more people will seek a slice of the cake and the proportion of each will be automatically reduced. To win systematically in such a game is no easier than in a casino. In addition the system is capable of detecting fraud, neutralising negative consequences and blocking abuses. This is possible because there is a whole range of defence mechanisms, based partly on the fact that much on the net reflects the offline world. Any single possession out of all those with which a person surrounds himself, viewed in isolation, might create a false impression of him, but taken together they do not lie. On the internet everything is just the same: ratings in the overall profile reflect a person's inner world, which is why it is not a simple matter to falsify them. One could of course make a determined effort and even achieve a measure of success, but not without incurring costs. It seems unlikely that many people will be seduced by ill-gotten gains of this kind.

The model of trust advertising is at the very least comparable in importance to the contextual advertising which has made internet search systems big business. Before the idea of selling contextual words to advertisers it was not clear how search engines could be monetised. As a result of this bright idea, a source of revenue appeared, in the wake of which search services grew explosively. The future of recommender systems lies in selling their basic goods, recommendations. Search and recommender services are complementary tools of the information society, the former providing access to information which the latter selects in accordance with subjective criteria. As soon as recommender services acquire their own business model, they will begin to rival search services in popularity.

So why has the idea of monetising networks through trust advertising not been thought of before? In part this is because the conventional leisure social networks, for all their high volumes of traffic, generate extremely meagre cash flows. We shall discuss this in the next section.

2.8.3 Prospects for Monetising Social Networks

Social networks on the internet have attracted vast amounts of attention. From the experience of contiguous branches of the media, this should represent a considerable commercial value when monetised with advertising. The question tormenting their owners is accordingly, "When will the networks start making decent money?" And what do they need to do in order to bring that about as soon as possible? Can profit in principle be extracted from social networks and, if so, why is it taking so long to happen? A secondary question of considerable interest is who this golden rain is going to fall on. Will it only be the owners and a few elite personages like popular bloggers who can look forward to becoming beneficiaries of the network, or can ordinary members also look forward to some profit?

Selling advertising, the business model of traditional media, has not so far proved very effective on social networks. The revenue collected has been infinitely less than in such other aggregators of attention as television or the press because the ultimate effectiveness of advertising on the networks is not particularly high. This reduces the cost of placing it. Moreover, users who get nothing out of it react badly to advertising, especially if it is placed on their personal pages without their consent. Aware of their importance for the network, they expect to be treated politely.

Throughout the world large numbers of bright people are puzzling over how to monetise social networks effectively, but it is becoming increasingly plain that for Web 2.0 sites there is no systemic solution. One can place advertising on general and personal pages; one can trade marketing information about users; one can charge them a fee to free them from inconveniences and restrictions one has first saddled them with. A little business can be done with highly rated bloggers and their postings. Money can be charged to display a photo in a prominent place. Virtual gifts and tokens of attention can be sold. There are a number of other ways of clipping the punters but so far none which yield the desired level of income.

While investors and a few professional bloggers are reaping a harvest of sorts, rank-and-file users of the networks have no prospect of earnings, yet these people contribute to the networks' value. They are jointly working up an information product. There is a contradiction here. Logically, the income of the networks and the income of its participants should be interconnected, and the one is not going to grow markedly while the other remains at zero. A firm which does not pay its employees will not prosper by relying solely on volunteers with their non-mercenary motivation. If a way could be found to pay users they would immediately start producing a vastly superior product and overall revenues would grow. But how can you enable users to earn if you can hardly make ends meet yourself? To rely upon generating income for some members of the group by taking it from others, as bookies do at the racecourse, is out of the question, against the ethos of the internet. Neither will it be possible to charge admission to newbies for arriving after all the work of setting up the network has been done. Each new recruit increases the value of the network, so it is unprofitable to raise entry barriers. Even just sharing the advertising revenue with participants of the network is problematical. At present there is, in any case, nothing much to share. The crumbs which would fall into the account of an ordinary user in recompense for displaying an advertisement several hundred or thousand times are not a game changer. It would be a different matter if we took the revenue of the entire network and shared it according to each participant's contribution, but this is not a Web 2.0 narrative, partly because it is unclear how the resources should be distributed. It could only be done by openly stratifying users, which would be risky. It is in any case pointless to talk about this at present, since averaged income divided among the total population of the network, even for the most visited sites, would barely add up to more than one dollar.

Of course, the earnings may not always be so meagre. It is no doubt indicative that the USA's Internal Revenue Service has taken steps to tax any income from the internet, thereby officially recognising that it is a place where private individuals earn income.

Let us allow ourselves a brief digression, since it concerns an important trend. As the internet becomes more commercialised, it is increasingly being subordinated to the offline world and obliged to play by rules established there. Initially the virtual world was seen by romantics as a sovereign space to which you could retreat, like a monastery, and live there according to your lights. Nobody could have anticipated how soon this specialness would begin to drain away. Copyright and endless offline lawsuits in connection with violations of copyright were the weapons which led to subjugation of the virtual territory. Although this course of events has to be regarded as predictable, there is a vague sense of a global dereliction of duty, and perhaps of a miracle which was never allowed to take place. It is as if the human race, having stumbled upon a highly promising discovery, decided not to take the risk of exploiting its potential but knuckled under to traditional rules and current vested interests, mainly commercial. These, as usual, crushed everything with the result that development is following a lower trajectory than it might have. Who knows, perhaps these regrets are premature and electronic networks will yet come into their own.

Social networks will not produce serious profits while they are based on Do-It-Yourself rather than creating a product for an external environment. If we take, for example, football in the street. Small boys do not get paid for kicking a ball around. Revenue only appears for those who play in front of grandstands and television cameras. Children would not be paid for playing in the sand unless they took to wearing advertisements on their T-shirts. Analogously, on today's social networks it is only the top talent which can earn anything, and they are not free to do what they want when they want to. This is the distinction between professional work and the amateur games currently in evidence on the social networks. It is a Rubicon which cannot be crossed by Web 2.0 sites. The prospect of earnings for rank-and-file users comes only with sites of the Web 3.0 generation, where users not only generate content but themselves certify it, thereby generating a product of vastly higher quality: information about the quality of goods and services. This is a facility beyond the means of today's best known social websites.

2.8.4 An Explanation of Demand and Unmediated Distribution

An inalienable part of the technology of collaborative filtering is the revelation of consumer opinion about the quality of goods and services. There is a royal road from this to commerce without middlemen. All distribution of goods is based on the proposition that the businesses and agents who form the links in the wholesale-retail chain possess increasingly detailed information about demand the closer they are to the end purchaser. The commercial agent makes his living from knowing what is required, and he risks acquiring a surplus of goods if his information proves inaccurate. Degrees of markup more largely reflect payment for information than for transport and warehousing logistics, technology, and financing the supply of goods. The efforts of producers to cater for every variety of taste and every individual requirement lead to an increase in the array of products on offer. This causes the price of knowledge about demand to rise, and increases the added value which middlemen bite off. Variety is by no means a free good. It was no whim of Henry Ford which dictated that every model-T coming off his conveyor belt should be black. The middle class emerging at that time could not have afforded a variety of different colours.

This was not because paint was expensive, but because of the overheads associated with wider choice. By comparison with standardised output, variety involves greater production costs and incomparably more expensive distribution because of the difficulty of predicting precisely how much of each product to manufacture and store. It is a fact of economics that the more modest the choice the lower the price. A bottle of beer chosen from 57 varieties set out on the counter will set you back twice as much as exactly the same bottle chosen from ten varieties. This is a universal logic which operates in every segment of the economy. To make matters worse, the varieties of different categories of goods have to be coordinated since a wide assortment of shirts makes no sense if there is a limited choice of ties. Significantly increasing choice makes everything an order of magnitude more expensive. If some particular category of demand is satisfied by a number of associated businesses manufacturing a restricted assortment then, allowing for their profit of 10–20% and the retail markup, the product will cost the retail customer around one-and-a half times the manufacturing cost. That was effectively the situation in the planned economy of the USSR. The retail prices we see today are several times more than the manufacturing cost. Incidentally, that is why it is a mistake to directly compare different economies in terms of GDP without rebasing them to a common denominator which takes account of variety, as is often done (perhaps deliberately) when comparing the present economy of Russia with that of the late Soviet period. Despite the fact that the GDP is formally the same, the contemporary situation is many times better and more effective. A command economy does not need to work so hard to feed and clothe everyone, outputting identical boots and margarine in large amounts. But actually it has not even the strength to do this, or more precisely, it lacks the motivation to put the strength it has into work.

Thanks to the recommender service, the needful information about demand will come directly from users, significantly weakening the need for middlemen. In a collaborative system you can see how many people have an interest in a particular item, which clarifies the ultimate demand for the producer, including demand which has not been satisfied by previous batches. This makes it possible to move to more economical schemes of shifting goods, like subscription, direct sales, and promoting new products with the aid of pioneer raters. Each has its own business model. The outcome will be a better coordination of supply and demand, a reduction of marketing costs, and possibly, most significantly, optimisation of choice by cutting back on the manufacture of products for which there is no demand, i.e., unsaleable goods. Double or even triple markup over factory cost is the price society is paying under the current distribution system for its love of choice. Direct feedback between producer and consumer promises to prove a valuable resource for economising on social costs. Economising is expected, then, to be possible firstly by dispensing with middlemen, secondly on the logistics of goods and money, and thirdly by partly replacing monetary settlement through the bartering of attention.

2.8.5 The Alternative to Copyright

In a number of areas the scheme of unmediated distribution is not only logical and timely, but also relatively easy to implement, with clear economies in all three of the aspects listed above: informational, logistical, and barter. These are the cinema, music, literature, the media and other digital industries, where there is no necessity for physical delivery or the prior creation and storage of an assortment of goods in case they are needed. This is precisely because the product is digitised. Today copyright rules OK in all these segments. As is to be expected in a world dependent on the movement of information, legislation regulating property rights to information plays a key role, but the traditional system of safeguarding authors' and associated rights is looking ever more out of date. It is time for a change.

Copyright is a bridge between art and commerce. It feeds both authors and commercial agents, manufacturers, publishers, impresarios. Production and distribution cannot dispense with any of them. The purpose of copyright is to block freeloaders and enable creative artists to harvest the fruits of their labour. Without copyright, commercial competitors would be free to pirate works created and launched by the hard work of somebody else, thereby taking a bite out of their legitimate income. This would discourage business people from becoming involved in cultural projects and lead to underproduction of the corresponding goods.

As we shall find out below, copyright serves mainly the interests of agents and middlemen, while we are talking about cutting out the middleman, an approach directly opposed to copyright. Let us try to understand the differing perspectives of these two systems. We will need to take a little time to understand the problems of copyright, which is arguably the most complicated and controversial law of modern times. Invented 300 years ago, it met the needs of its age, but since then circumstances have changed and there are many grievances. Let us briefly list them.

1. Copyright has made business people the main players in culture and has, moreover, led to the appearance of monopolists who inflate the price of cultural production. People do not want to pay way over the odds for songs which in their (not entirely informed) belief cost nothing to produce and are easily copied.

2. The major corporations oppress authors, do not pay them properly, and prey on them.
3. In the past, copyright regulated a modest part of cultural production. Today, when peer-to-peer (file exchange) networks have created the opportunity for mass evasion of copyright, the law has been made more draconian in reaction. People continue nevertheless to exchange works hand to hand (as if this were occurring in a family circle, only one which has just become infinitely extended). Rights holders everywhere see a threat to their income, and on that basis demand total monitoring to see whether anybody has copied anything illegally, even if that means violating people's privacy, since the rights holders treat everyone as potential criminals. Protection of some rights leads to violation of other, more vital, rights and freedoms.
4. Copyright has been extended to derivative items, with the result that every fragment of a text can be registered as somebody's property. A work is not born in a vacuum, however. It has to start from something achieved in the past and known to the public. It transpires, however, that everything belongs to someone and you have to haggle for permission to use it. This creates artificial barriers to creativity. Creative artists who have forged ahead of the field and are already established are protected, but all those behind them are mistreated. This works in the interests of narrow groups and to the detriment of culture.
5. It is often difficult to understand what can be lifted and under what circumstances, which leads to violation of the law through ignorance. Copyright law has opened the way to lawsuits in every connection, and in these disputes power is naturally on the side of the corporations. This unties their hands.
6. Copyright was created in order to stimulate creativity economically, but in fact it makes life more difficult for creative people (with the exception of stars). Thanks to copyright, businesses have taken possession of the whole corpus of creative artists' rights and have consolidated to a point where in each sector they can be counted on one's fingers (for example, there are four principal majors in sound recording). The creative artist cannot afford not to play by the corporation's rules and it dictates the terms. All that can be created is what the corporation is prepared to promote. Nothing else, with rare exceptions, gets into production.
7. Copyright does not protect the property interests of authors. No matter what may be written in the law, royalties are determined in the course of negotiations with the producer, or in this case the publisher, and here, with the exception of superstars, the situation places the author at a disadvantage. Should he prove obstreperous, others can be found to replace him. It is impossible to live without earnings for long and there are very few other corporations to turn to. As a result, creative artists are underpaid.
8. The law was passed in an age when poverty meant that by no means all talented people could afford to create. Under these conditions, economic stimulation of investment in culture was justified. Today no incentive is required: those striving to express themselves creatively are legion. In earlier times there was a hunger for content and the information space needed to be filled. Now it is

overfull, while a mechanism, devised to ensure further consolidation, continues to operate.

As we see, there are no few grievances on a variety of levels. Masses of people, feeling that the law is unjust, break it. Piracy would not be so ubiquitous if it did not have support among the people. Copyright is now in marked conflict with its initial goals. Should society use copyright to continue protecting the earnings from culture of a few small groups against the interests of the many? The contradiction is evident and will not go away.

Copyright does, however, have its defenders. They argue that without business support a creative artist has no chance of gaining the widespread recognition for which he thirsts. The maxim beloved of art connoisseurs, "Genius will out," is empty without a market presence. The creative artist cannot do without the businessman, and the latter will not take up the cudgels unless he is sure that the fruits of his labours are under his control and will not be filched by somebody else. The author turns to an agent for support at a time when nobody knows whether there is money to be made. The agent agrees to take part in a risky venture only on condition that, if things go well, he will get his cut. The aim of copyright is to ensure this. The fact is that the publisher, like a merchant, takes on the risk of correctly guessing what is going to be a saleable commercial proposition in the future and in return wants to have a firm right to the income. Abolishing copyright is tantamount to doing away with the intermediary. If we are to take this matter seriously, we need to ask the question, "How can we get by without a publisher?"

The apologists' second argument is that opponents of copyright underestimate the contribution of business. They are not in possession of information about the true costs and mistakenly believe that publishers are fleecing the artist. In accordance with the market norm, an author can expect under his contract 10–20% of the revenue. At first sight this division seems unfair. One in five or one in ten: the author's take seems pretty slim. That 10–20%, however, is being paid to a successful or, more exactly, profitable author. In the majority of cases authors are unprofitable. They bring the publisher losses which he has to recoup from profitable projects. It can be said that successful authors rescue unsuccessful authors through the mediation of the publisher. The widespread opinion that authors are being paid too little and businessmen are taking too much is incorrect: taking account of loss-making projects, the income is being divided more or less fairly.

Although in the minds of most people copyright was invented for authors, in fact what it really does is incentivise entrepreneurs. The institution was from the outset conceived as rigorously commercial. Questions of morality and concern for the creative artist are far from being at the forefront. In the first law of copyright (Statute of Anne, 1710) there is no mention of authors at all. The topic is exclusively the rights of the publisher.

And yet, no matter what arguments are put forward, people cannot get their heads round all those agents' cuts. Most would like to see creative artists paid more and the product costing less. The only way this is possible is through a radical reduction of distribution costs, which is what we are coming to. Under the existing technology, the producer model of culture costs society a sum consisting of production and promotion costs. If public opinion agrees that the producer is getting too much and artists too little, while the customer is paying too much, it is possible to try to do without producers. It is, however, impossible simply to decide to remove them from the chain of production. Somebody has to take on their work, which is principally the selection and promotion of talented artists, and also their other functions, and to do it all for less money.

We thus arrive logically at the unmediated scheme and at group filtering. A first attempt to implement this was made in 1999 in the celebrated Napster project. With the aid of file exchange networks (a brilliant invention thanks to which users are able directly to exchange interesting content) Napster intended to identify and promote musicians through the efforts of listeners. Realisation of the plan was prevented by a lawsuit which closed down the site for copyright infringement. It has to be said that, even if this had not happened, one essential link for success was in any case missing, namely a selection mechanism. Many aspire to fame, and there has to be a way of deciding what each hopeful is worth. Otherwise, a promising performer risks being swamped, and the consumer risks being drowned, by myriad graphomaniacal opuses, some of which might possibly appeal to him if he ever got to see them. There was also no answer to the question of how performers were to be paid. It was assumed that, having gained a reputation on the internet, they would make their fortune beyond its boundaries on the basis of increased demand for their concerts.

Technologically, then, the internet was ready for unmediated commerce 10 years ago. Everything ground to a halt because of the absence of two mechanisms crucial to the New Economy: (1) end-user evaluation with the aid of collaborative filtering; (2) post-factum gratuity payment able to provide creative artists with an income. Consumers have only to get used to acting as patrons of the arts, and begin voluntarily paying for the products they have enjoyed, to discover that they need pay only one third of the current retail price. The unmediated electronic scheme reduces the cost of the product many times, and that is the social benefit which is at stake. Moreover, the artist will be paid two if not three times as much as at present and additional sales will be delivered by collaborative filtering, which can identify a latent niche market. If people genuinely, and not just declaratively, are concerned for their favourite artists, if they truly are so opposed to copyright, they will adopt the post-factum scheme. To summarise what has been said, we will see that we have a valid alternative to copyright. Of the three essential components, two are already to hand: e-commerce is expanding ever more widely, and a recommender service based on collaborative filtering is functioning. The next step is voluntary post factum payment but, heaven knows, it would be difficult to imagine better conditions for making a start with this practice than e-commerce with digital content.

No matter how controversial copyright may be, in the present economy a lot hinges on it. Accordingly, it is naive to suppose that people will voluntarily give the institution up, or that there can be some forcible solution to the problem. (If such a thing is possible, then it will most likely end in favour of copyright.) It is very revealing that in 2002 a group of 17 highly eminent scientists, including five Nobel prize winners in economics, addressed objections to the Supreme Court of the USA to the extending of the period of copyright at the instigation of Disney Studios. (In the course of the last century it has been extended dozens of times, whenever the copyright period of representations of Mickey Mouse was about to expire.) The signatories claimed that the extension was economically senseless and harmful to culture, but their arguments were not accepted. Other, also authoritative, economists were found who put forward directly contrary arguments, and these were specialists in legal economics, among them Stan J. Liebowitz, Stephen E. Margolis, William M. Landes and Richard A. Posner.

This example confirms that the fate of copyright will be decided not so much in debates as through market competition with the institution of user evaluation and unmediated commerce. With the growth of direct links between artists and their public, the need for mediators, and correspondingly for copyright, will weaken. It may be strategically advantageous for a beginning artist to reject copyright. If he has talent, he will attract attention on the internet and be promoted to a prominent position. Those able to gain fairly wide popularity will find themselves in the ideal situation of being their own masters, obliged to no one for anything. Today it has somehow been forgotten that creative artists do actually have a place in the practice of copyright. Without their initial agreement to concede copyright to corporations there would be nothing there. However, up to the present time this "unconditional surrender" is inescapable because of the lack of other ways of earning an income and building a career. When there is an alternative, artists will be able to decide for themselves which approach is better for them. Stars who have made their name within the framework of the old system will probably not change, but for the rest there are good grounds to try the unmediated approach, knowing that they are not risking anything. For example, authors of highbrow books are today unable to live on their literary earnings. The print run of books is wretched and the royalties correspondingly low. Physical distribution lags behind, because it is impossible to service a tiny, geographically dispersed demand, even if it is known to be there. An author will lose little if he moves to internet distribution with post-payment. He stands to gain an immeasurably greater public than he would with a paper book, and it is likely to be better targeted. Having agreed a direct contract with his public, the author could go on to become the senior partner in an alliance with a publisher. Quite unexpectedly they may exchange roles, and it will not be the publisher benignly tossing royalties to the author, but the author employing the services of a producer.

2.9 The Topology of Taste

2.9.1 Group Recommendations and the Love of Reading

While analysing the diverse practices and institutions growing out of collaborative filtering, it will be as well to remind ourselves that they are built on a solid foundation. We would be shirking our duty if we ignored a problem which challenges collaborative technology itself, namely, making recommendations in a situation where taste is changing. The basic algorithm for computing recommendations uses a profile compiled from rating of goods which a person has consumed at different periods of his life. Over this time his taste may have changed, and assessments from long ago may no longer reflect who he is today. Likewise, ratings given today may not correspond with an impression made in the past. His interests may have changed. If we do not take countermeasures, this will lead to faulty recommendations. For users with established tastes, the problem is quite easily resolved: outdated ratings are firmly separated from recent ones. If taste is evolving rapidly, however, as happens in childhood, youth and, not infrequently, adulthood too, the computing of recommendations becomes far more difficult. Today's algorithms do not cope with these subtleties, neither collaborative algorithms (for the present) nor any others. Moreover, the problem has not been posed in these terms anywhere in the world. In order to resolve it, we need to select for the user not just counterparts in his group with analogous ratings, but also to extract from that selection people who are at the same stage of taste development. In terms of psychology, it is a matter of hitting the proximate circle of development. In other words, it is desirable that what is recommended should not be too simple, since otherwise it will be boring, and not so complex that the user will give up in despair. Developing motivation and interest is the subtlest element in personal development. Today it is unduly dependent on the quality of one's instructor, and luck.

Let us take as an example adolescents' reluctance to read. The problem is constantly discussed, but without any very obvious conclusions being reached. A majority of children read under duress because they don't find reading interesting. The books adults urge upon them are what the adults found absorbing when they were young, but today they are incapable of enticing many away from the monitor. School reading lists contain a dazzling, polished corpus of texts, but they are not exactly pageturners.

Collaborative technology can enable us to generate a qualitatively different offering of literature. It is necessary to identify users, preferably of the same age group, who have read the same books in the same sequence and moved on to the next stage. Works which gripped them in this phase slightly ahead of the user's present development are the ones children should be advised to read. Then one should put one's money not only on the fact that a book is good. That is not enough. It needs also a well chosen context of perception, as positive experience of advisers tells us. Mathematically, the task comes down to calculating the proximity of trajectories along which taste has progressed, and this is more difficult than establishing a similarity between collections of numbers which characterise the tastes of users. It is essential to detect similarity between series of ratings. This task is not elementary, but very promising, and resolving it will lead to a breakthrough both in the field of recommender algorithms and in educational technologies. Not only literature and the whole sphere of culture, but also mathematics, natural science, history, chess, and other areas are in urgent need of finding "itineraries" of tasks, balanced between the coordinates of interest and ability. In all cases it is of fundamental importance to hit the proximate circle of development. An automated selection of appropriate study material will make it possible to alleviate one of the most acute problems of the present system, a levelling approach to teaching. This is a problem not only for school education but also for the self-education of mature people, who can find it very difficult to master a new area.

Experiments with developing tastes will help us to find the key to one other very old problem: how to objectively determine quality in art without relying on "authorities." Although today the topic of a hierarchy of artistic quality is avoided (not least because of an injection of post-modernism), deep in the heart of many people the hope springs that quality does in fact exist (as does a lack of it) and that some day it will be possible to argue this out rigorously. The collaborative mechanism already allows us to replace the question of, "What is quality?" with the questions, "Who considers this high quality?" and "For whom is this a work of quality?" "What" becomes "who." When we teach the collaborative system to weigh up who is who in the symbolic realm, it will be possible to return to this question of a hierarchy of artistic quality. For the time being it is customary in the art system to rely on tables of rank compiled within the professional community. The problem is that these hierarchies often turn out to be politicised or constructed in accordance with extraneous interests remote from culture. A recommender system makes it possible to overcome these snags.

2.9.2 Encouraging Good Taste

Even a brief analysis of the dynamics of taste allows us to dispel the worry which critics voice from time to time that recommendations supposedly lead to a conservation of tastes and slow down their development. In doing so the critics base themselves on the following erroneous postulate: since the exchange of opinions is occurring between people of a similar circle, there is no opportunity for growth. The reality is quite the opposite. Collaborative technology does not level taste down to the level of the weakest but draws it upwards. People, when they are given the opportunity of choosing the best, do in fact prefer the best. It would be strange in that situation to choose what has been rejected. From experience of the functioning of collaborative sites, it can be said clearly that nobody behaves in this way. Accordingly, the system of group selection works as an incubator of taste.

To stretch a point somewhat, perception of a work of art can be characterised in terms of complexity. This complexity is of roughly the same kind as that of chess compositions. Solving a problem to his taste, a person experiences aesthetic pleasure, and in the process trains his taste and acquires artistic competence, which in turn prompts him to solve more and more complex problems and promises new helpings of pleasure. With the growth of complexity, the muscles of taste are toned up, while long periods of neglect lead to a loss of fitness in taste. It loses its edge and degrades. Accordingly, even just blocking the worst and pointing to the best has a beneficial effect on taste.

Despite the fact that experience is being exchanged within a taste community, its members are not clones and do not consume the same thing at the same time. If some addict of fantasy gives a high rating to, say, the Russian art movie "Cloud paradise," he will bring it to the attention of the rest of his circle. Similarly, a blockbuster fan has only to receive pleasure from essays about life in ancient Rome for this automatically to become available to his taste neighbours and their friends.

The problem of cocooning is thus purely imaginary. When people exchange quality experience, the average level invariably rises. We should remember too that the system does not confine anybody within the walls of a mechanically selected reference group. If you wish, you can take a closer look at the interests of other groups and people. The partitions are entirely porous. You can inspect the choice of others with whom you have coincidences in rated works, and you can read professional criticism (fortunately, recommender systems are capable of identifying critics who are closest to a particular user). Collaborative filtering makes models deserving of emulation visible, which is an important way to develop good taste. It is similar to what takes place in computer games: it simply doesn't happen that a person for no reason decides to regress from an advanced level to the beginners' level. Everybody climbs upwards, and the fact that you can choose your own pace is decidedly helpful. A recommender service delivers the same kind of progression.

2.10 The New Economy is an Economy of Clubs

Let us summarise what has been said in Chap. 2.

The prospects for society are closely tied to the development of group life. The link is not obvious, but extremely important. The quality of life both of the individual and of society as a whole is directly dependent on how effective the tools are for forming groups, clubs and communities. Many problems are solved by organising groups within a community. This is why the tools for forming them are so important and why the prospects for third generation social networks are so promising. Creating new mechanisms and institutions for group building is at the top of today's agenda, and everything reviewed in the present volume relates in one way or another to that topic.

A club is a group of people who are in some way of interest to each other, with whom a person can find shared priorities and enthusiasms and thereby realise his own potential. The discovery of such groups, joining them, participating in them is both a goal and reason for living for each of us. It is a path to personal happiness because this is how people come to self-realisation, by raising the quality of their communication. They meet other worthwhile people in the context of issues which matter to them and thereby manage the quality of their time. Improving that is the true aim of a human being. Groups are also a way of balancing the interests of society and the individual. They enable a person to acquire a comfortable environment and shield himself from uncongenial people.

The New Economy serves the acute social need for stratification, differentiation and association. If we understand this we can gain a proper appreciation of the lifestyle it offers. The process of differentiation, with an institution supporting it, is in the interests of each and every one of us, since everybody feels the need to associate with his own kind of people and be apart from outsiders. He wants to belong, but he also wants to be an individual. The New Economy provides all that is needed for forming the strata, groups, communities, circles, associations and so on which a finely structured society requires. All its industries work towards producing attributes and signs of differentness which aid division into groups. This enables each person to position himself in society, to find a niche corresponding to the level he is on and in which, accordingly, he is comfortable. Today's priority is to provide the individual with tools so that he can search out those with whom he will be at ease, and help him to associate with them. How can this be facilitated? The answer is to be found in the new technologies and practices of communication.

Web networks offer rich opportunities for forming associations. The fact that the groups are now virtual does not make them any less viable, nor any less real and useful. My view is that one of the most promising and revolutionary tools is group (collaborative) filtering. It has always existed, although under different names, but in social networks it has reached a new level of efficiency. The mechanism is part and parcel of a new way of ordering the world through groups, which is why it is so central in this book. Group filtering is a means for people to interact and find each other, to come together and cooperate for their mutual benefit. There are numerous examples of such fruitful associations functioning on different levels and different scales, from tiny niche communities of shared tastes and interests to very large groups indeed, including political groupings. The benefits people derive from coming together can be extremely varied, but collective filtering of information and material goods and services promises the highest return. It increases the efficiency of individual consumer choice while, on a completely different, institutional level, organising a link between production and consumption and providing the feedback mechanism any social activity needs.

Thanks to group filtering the individual acquires a new degree of freedom and society is far more harmoniously structured than previously. This is a means of raising the quality of life, since each person has the opportunity to find his own congenial microworld, something it is far more difficult to create in other ways. The costs on this path are substantially reduced by the new tools, institutions and business models discussed in this volume: collective filtering, unmediated links, post factum gratuity payments (capable of becoming an alternative to copyright), mutually regulated group behaviour, insurance of experience (cultural) goods, symbolic exchange without money (attention bartering), and trust advertising.

Chapter 3
The Symbolic Economics Approach to the Humanities and Humanitarian Practices

3.1 Prospects for Humanities Research into Third-Generation Networks

3.1.1 Measuring Symbolic Exchange

A little over half a century ago the study of history was given a powerful boost when the *Annales* school engaged in studying the economies of past eras. On the basis of archive data a start was made at that time on recreating, piece by piece, a picture of material exchange in order to investigate the distribution of wealth, the growth of institutions and the structure of markets. The result was a more complete understanding of the moving forces of history. Today's priority is quantitative measurement of non-material processes. Without this our understanding of many phenomena is guesswork, and we can only shrug vaguely when asked for precise forecasting of choices society will face. Until recently attempts to calculate anything in the arts got nowhere because we lacked any halfway usable instruments of measurement, but now internet technologies enable us to tear aside the curtain concealing the quantitative parameters of symbolic exchange. There is nothing to keep us from moving from talk to action apart from a firmly rooted conviction that this is beyond our capacity. If thinking in the humanities moves in this direction it can look forward to a new upward spiral of development: if it does not, it faces stagnation.

The only place substantial progress has been made is in information economics, where it is beginning to be understood that attention is a resource (Herbert Simon). In the process, science is on the verge of introducing quantitative methods in the symbolic field. However, there continues to be a lack of important data about the

A. Dolgin, *Manifesto of the New Economy*,
DOI 10.1007/978-3-642-21277-2_3, © The Author(s) 2012

quantity and quality of information. The quantity can be more or less estimated, but what is to be done about the quality of information? There are no outward signs, professional judgements are scrappy and contradictary, and market indicators can prove deceptive. Science encounters similar difficulties even when merely measuring conventional utilitarian values. These too cannot be coordinated while they are in people's minds, until they turn up in the marketplace and become manifest through willingness to pay for exchanges, through prices. Symbolic values cannot be measured in this way. For a number of reasons, then, it is not easy to quote them in monetary terms, even if we look to the markets. I have written in detail about this in my book *The Economics of Symbolic Exchange*. As an example, let me recall the paradox of uniform prices, when movies, books and sound recordings of entirely different quality are all sold at the same price. To some extent the value of the symbolic can be arrived at indirectly through calculation of the time, memory and attention which are condensed in a particular text, but this is a tortuous and thorny path which still does not bring the desired clarity. A number of significant factors remain unconsidered, some which precede the exchange (preferences, desires and motivations) and also some which follow from it (emotions, new meanings and satisfaction).

It cannot be said that the social sciences ignore exchange processes, or that people in the humanities find it difficult to use the corresponding terminology. Economic historians, for example, sociologists, political scientists and others analyse events using the categories of symbolic gain and loss which motivate interest groups, but these are on a purely verbal level. There is a total absence of numerical quantification of the concept of exchange, and that is the only thing which makes an exchange approach truly productive. When people talk importantly about "exchange", when they explain so much by it, one would like to know what the stakes are, what is being exchanged for what and in what proportions. Alas, the parities involved in symbolic exchange could not be detected even recently. With few exceptions, data had to be scratched around for and pecked out a grain at a time. There was simply nowhere the data could be found in the necessary quantities. The richest source of information about non-utilitarian exchange was the markets of culture, but what they clarify is mainly what can be detected through monetary indicators. The box office shows us only the tip of the symbolic iceberg, that part which falls within the purview of commerce. This includes antiques, classical music, collectables, and anything else associated with scarcity. The rest, like poetry, goes unconsidered and yet, although free, some of it is priceless. What little we know about the value of leisure and attention is thanks to the advertising markets where these resources are traded more or less transparently for money. It is, however, the exception when money is a relevant indicator of value in the symbolic field.

It is sometimes possible to derive data indirectly from market indicators by using calculations based on a number of assumptions. Thus, the symbolic value of collecting art can be estimated if we track how far the potential revenue from selling pictures lags behind the return on investing in bonds. We find that canvases appreciate in value over time more slowly than gilts. Collectors are accordingly forfeiting income and their losses can be viewed as payment for the right to enjoy art, a monetary equivalent of the value of collecting. When serfs in Russia were to be punished for their misdemeanours they would be offered a choice between being whipped or paying a fine. This is convenient for the economist because it clearly defines the price of non-acceptance of violence, although our stoical forebears on the whole chose to be whipped. Such distinct tariffs are rare. The markets in sport, medicine, and war also give some understanding of the monetary equivalents of values in the humanities, but it is far from complete. On the whole, money and markets are poor quantifiers of non-utilitarian values.

As far as identifying the proportions on each side was concerned, symbolic exchange until recently bore no comparison with material exchange. Now, however, its contours are visible and it seems likely that in the near future it will be numerically quantifiable. Social networks on the internet are where the pattern of non-material exchange is to be found. Networks have drawn in a significant proportion of human activity and, importantly, have codified it. Internet groups are an excellent model for researching the whole of society, not only because in many respects they copy real life, but also because the processes which occur in them do not need to be processed: they are already in the form of postings and the structured actions of users. Huge numbers of people leave traces on the internet of what they are doing in their lives, both online and offline. These indicate not only the event and date but also come with emotional colouration which, in third-generation networks, is overtly expressed in ratings and points awarded. This provides an opportunity to measure resources input, for example the time spent on communicating in a social network, and to see the resultant output expressed in the user's subjective rating. Web 3.0 sites allow us to observe the reaction to actions and objects not only on the internet but also in the outside world. The action occurs in reality, while the consumer's attitude to it is registered on the site. Internet activity does not, of course, reveal life in all its fullness, but it is an excellent testing ground. From the flow of internet transactions data can be extracted which is of interest to a wide spectrum of sciences like sociology, political science, psychology, cultural studies, art history, linguistics and institutional and behavioural economics. What historians fish out of archives and sociologists from questionnaires will swim of its own accord into nets for researchers to harvest. Possibly the richness of the networks will engender that interdisciplinarity on which so many hopes have been pinned for so long.

Values are in people's minds and become manifest in the course of exchange. The fuller and more visible the exchange, the more detailed the statistics about acts of exchange, the more clearly will we be able to see what people are prepared to part with in order to acquire a particular good or service.

At the risk of repeating ourselves, the sole means of measuring values is to place them in conditions of intensive, remunerated exchange, that is a market. Exchange processes in networks are moving towards the market model, but as communications become more dense, and when in the future the internet, television, and telephone communication all converge on a single platform, these exchange processes will occur ever more plainly in accordance with market laws. At the same time, the proportions of symbolic exchange will crystallise out and become particularly evident with the introduction of post factum payments and monetisation of social networks generally. In the Stone Age too it was not immediately clear how many bananas should be exchanged for a clay pot. Having once begun, the calibration of exchange correlations will become irreversible. When even a small part of what we know about material exchange has accumulated, this will have a powerful influence on awareness of tariffs of symbolic exchange and will ricochet to affect the course of actual processes. At this stage the second invisible hand of the market will begin to act, in accordance with fundamentally different principles. Like Adam Smith's invisible hand, its main driver is data about the observable acts of participants.

Without a doubt, we will shortly learn to extract a mass of useful information from the rich seam of logged human communication on the internet, even if today analysts do not quite know how to approach the task. There is, of course, the highly sensitive question of what we want to learn about people and life from the internet. Users seem to be producing actions, moving like Brownian particles under a microscope, but we are not sure what we should be looking for. This is probably why the predominant research approach is to view users as potential customers. At least this makes it clear who will fund the research. Works on the economics of the internet and social networks, however, can be counted on your fingers. Everything that can be found on this topic was written in the last millennium when networks as they exist today were simply not there. The sociology of social networks has also not advanced far beyond corporative marketing, with its emphasis on delivering targeted sales.

To summarise, let us return to our principal thesis: everything is now in place for quantitative measurement of symbolic exchange. It is essential to focus the various research forces on the internet, since that is where a convenient bridgehead has appeared for making a breakthrough. Timely as this call undoubtedly is, it will not be enough on its own to move things forward. If exchange is conducted by barter, as it mainly is on social networks, the quantitative parameters we are looking for will be difficult to detect; and if for money, the measurements, as we have already noted, introduce more confusion than clarity. We will next need to resolve the issue of a unit of measurement of symbolic value, without which our intentions will not be fully realisable. We shall return to this a few chapters from now. For the present, though, let us just partly show our hand: symbolic exchange can be represented in numbers by measuring the input and output of what drives it: the transformation of objective time into subjective personal value. A person seeks to exchange the time at his disposal for something which will bring meaning to his existence and evoke a positive reaction in his mental make up, whether by socialising, reading or study. We can characterise this transformation generally by modifying the renowned formula about capital to read: "time–text–time*", where "*" signifies the increased quality time, and "text" stands for any symbolic product in objective form. In this formula "text" occupies the same place and plays the same role as "money" in Marx's formula "goods–money–goods", mediating the transformation of goods into better goods. Just as money accumulates capital in itself, so texts accumulate symbolic capital. Those two kinds of capital can be exploited with variable effectiveness, an understanding of which is facilitated by traditional or symbolic economics respectively. In the social networks the general idea of symbolic exchange assumes concrete form: who is exchanging what with whom, in what proportions, at what moment in time. All this extremely valuable empirical evidence is there, waiting to be collected and analysed.

3.1.2 Studying Dissemination of Information

The next major topic after measurement of exchange is the dissemination of information. Of utmost importance in the information society are signals and the mechanisms by which they are spread: their points of origin, their power, their trajectories, their duration and geographical coverage. Understanding the spread of information is even more difficult than measuring exchange, and of equal practical importance. Whereas the correlations to be observed in exchange are by and large static, here, by definition, everything is dynamic. Here too, however, electronic, especially third-generation, social networks offer a new and very promising book-keeping tool, since the information they contain is both registered and processed in vastly greater detail, while the communications themselves are organised in a more complex manner. By comparison with ordinary networks with their blogger potpourri of actual postings and comments or quotations, a Web 3.0 network contains far more valuable data. There are personalised profiles, collections of ratings behind which a subject with a name and surname is visible, along with his socio-demographic characteristics and consumer history. In brief, there is a full-blown cultural anamnesis. On Web 2.0 sites it is usual for ratings, if they are collected at all, to be confined to a narrow range of topics from which no overall understanding of the user's preferences can be formed. With Web 3.0, however, each of these reflections comes with a precise date, so that any action can be analysed in the context of other actions, and any rating within a system of other ratings. By monitoring network communications we can detect, for example, the moment and place in society where particular processes appear, who takes them up and why, by which routes and at what speed they spread. This enables us to track the dissemination of social awareness deep inside society rather than relying on the sociological samples or media voxpops which currently have to serve.

At one time the consumer had the choice of objects with various pluses and minuses, but when a certain level of social prosperity was reached, the social signalling function of objects, how they were perceived by those around, began to outweigh their directly utilitarian functions. Relations between the real and the perceived became more complex until a point was reached where signs became an end in themselves and capable of overshadowing and manipulating realities. They can easily signify something which does not actually exist, or which is at variance with reality. These are so-called simulacra. They are almost given official permission to bear false witness. The same applies to signals: they can refer to non-existent or wantonly interpreted signs, processes or events. (By "signs" we are referring here to something which contains information, and by "signals" to whatever transmits it.) Just as signs can be more important than the actual nature of things, so signals can prove almost more important than the facts they make known.

The greater the importance of communications in our lives, the more significant do the treatment and ways of disseminating information become. Often, correctly presented information can be decisive. It programs subsequent behaviour. Signals can be transmitted selectively and interpreted arbitrarily to produce a reaction in the masses not based on an objective understanding and hence difficult to foresee. Networks enable us to track the routes taken by information not in general but individually, literally person by person, and equally individually to register their reaction. In the past there was no way of approaching this problem and, until it could be solved, humanity had no prospect of making progress in its desire to reduce the uncertainty of the future.

It can be sufficient to show people a new truth about themselves for whole classes to start behaving differently. The material preconditions have to be present, of course, but they are never sufficient on their own; skilled interpretation is more important than anything else, as Marx and Lenin demonstrated in practice. Why confine ourselves to ideology, though? A century and a half ago it took Pasteur decades to inculcate new standards of hygiene. People either believed him or they didn't, and depending on that they washed or did not wash their hands. If convictions were that important in Pasteur's non-ideological issues, which were a matter of life and death, how influential must they be in the New Economy where mind is so plainly influential over matter. Attitudes towards youth, age, beauty, charity, the upbringing of children, contemporary art, money-lending, dissidents and so on all result from work on consciousness, to some extent purposeful and in the service of particular interests, and to some extent spontaneous and not specifically managed by anybody.

For example, attempts are being made in developing countries to establish the boundaries of a middle class, which is seen as promoting stability and prosperity. An effective move would be to devise the portrait of this stratum in such a way as to include as many social groupings as possible. A mere reclassification by the media would allow people who believed themselves poor to take a step up the ladder in their own eyes and would thereby help them on to the strait and narrow path of consumerism. Teachers drag hopeless pupils tottering on the verge of failure up into the next class in the knowledge that they have only to believe in themselves for a powerful updraft to be engaged, which will grow even more powerful as they approach a goal which had initially appeared unattainable. Inner motivation is the key to understanding the effectiveness of signals, even when they are flattering or deceptive. Where there is information competition, everything depends on who proves more convincing and whose initiative is taken up first. A signal given at the right moment programs expectations and these materialise in a willingness to rally round particular initiatives, to contribute or withhold one's energy (vote), and accordingly to influence the outcome. People feel a need to take their place in processes where what matters most is not "what?", but "who with?".

At the present time we know in only general terms about the dissemination of information in society. This does not let opinion-formers of various kinds off the hook of being expected to manage social perception. To a large extent they are flying by the seat of their pants and naturally make mistakes in abundance. There is no point in blaming anybody for this, since people always have a measure of freedom which introduces unpredictability into how they will react to a particular message. For example, in a period of financial crisis you need to be certain, when deciding whether to inject money into the economy, that citizens will increase consumption and not just decide to hoard resources for a rainy day. Alas, a government can only guess because there is no unambiguous advice in works on macroeconomics. Even less are there hints on how to nudge public reaction in the desired direction. We cannot boast even a framework for understanding dynamic information processes. Public opinion can turn one way or the other depending on how information is presented. A barrage of unfavourable commentaries, and even what seem to be the most reasonable decisions, taken in full accordance with available theory, may have the opposite effect to what was anticipated. Then again, moves which the same theory suggests are highly unpromising may prove successful.

Judging by the relatively smooth course of the 2008–2009 crisis, jobbing economists have been able to put out the seats of the fire. The Russian government selectively helped national corporations to settle with their foreign creditors, saving them from facing "margin calls" (a forced sale of securities at knockdown prices). Public perception of the move tended to be negative. Supporting favourites with state funds when others were not provided with similar resources was indeed morally questionable. Nevertheless, these and a number of other demonstrative measures, signalling firm if not fully implemented intentions, produced the desired results. Bankers took note of the signal and did not start demanding the repayment of debts as vigorously as they might have. The threatened avalanche of margin calls was successfully averted.

Politics is largely a matter of management through the creation of legends and leaks. That is what it does, getting the millstones to grind with a minimal input of effort. The theory of how this works is embryonic, but elaborating it would enable us in future to reduce the role of political instinct and improve the quality of calculation. At present the dissemination of information is at best something going on in people's minds. Serious modelling is far beyond our current capability and only game theory is working on this. In public debate about the failure of a particular project we never hear mention of the dissemination or lack of it, reliability or lack of it, or the fullness or lack of it of information. The reason is only too obvious: a lack of theoretically grounded arguments. There is not even any halfway accepted vocabulary current in society to ensure that the whole area is not regarded as pure hocus-pocus. The result is that complex matters are outrageously simplified, with no account taken of important factors. That is damaging. While everything is at this level of tight-lipped oniscience we can only passively observe the swirling of the great sea of events in society. By and large, nobody will be able to make any sense of either minor upsets or global social cataclysms. We will have to make do with commentary with the benefit of hindsight.

Precise, systematic data about the dissemination of information can be extracted from Web 3.0 social networks and, as of now, from nowhere else. Not, at least, in the quantities we are looking for. Researchers face a number of difficulties as they wrestle with multiple interconnections between reality, attitudes towards reality, and information about those attitudes. The superimposition of accretions of differing levels of complexity will afflict them with that same sense of never being able to get a handle on anything as affected the philosophers of the School of Athens.

The situation is reminiscent of the spy game "I know that you know that I know...", which even game theory seems unable to get to grips with. This is especially the case in practical instances when it really is not known who is informed to what extent about what other participants know. For all that, no matter how intricate the game appears, it is never too difficult to be mastered by the strongest players, who are able to see through weaker partners. For all its labyrinthine complexity, the system is not unfathomable. Two seams can be separated out: the views or standpoints which directly determine actions, and what influences those views.

We are primarily interested in one, possibly the most important, aspect of this influence which derives from the group nature of the structure of society. People initially react to new facts (or what they are told about them) to the extent that they impinge on their own private interests. In the course of subsequent private and public communications, individual positions become aggregated and adapt themselves to group platforms. It is important to understand how and why this happens. Personal interests alter both as a result of new understanding of a situation, but also as a result of observing which platforms are most rapidly acquiring supporters and becoming viable. There are two crucial influences at work here. The first is which facts are made public and how they are presented, what is made made known and what is kept quiet. The second, and most important, is how much information people have about the potential number of supporters particular interest groups have which they might consider joining, and also how many supporters the groups currently have and how fast their ranks are growing. As regards the filtering of information, the principle is well enough understood because a number of stratagems have long been in use for manipulating society's choices. Nevertheless, how the information cascade operates and the pathways it follows remain unknown. In order to understand how people act in particular circumstances, we need to know not only their attitude to those circumstances and their assessment of the likely final relative strength of various forces, but also the information they had when they made their decision and the extent to which they were following the herd. Figuratively speaking, what odds are they anticipating when they gamble on a particular group winning? This question is similarly posed in game theory.

The inversion of Marx's dictum to read "consciousness determines being" (or analogously, "mind over matter") has become a commonplace frequently used in discussions of mind games where thinking is unfettered by logic. But what determines mind? For as long as the informational substratum in which personal and social principles mature remains unresearched, the phrase "consciousness determines...", which appears to explain something, is a mere smokescreen. Until it can be translated into numbers, it will remain as impenetrable as the word "exchange" used to be.

The two most promising directions for humanities research into social networks are, then:

- Quantitative research into symbolic exchange
- Analysis of the dissemination of information

3.1.3 Modelling Group and Network Effects

Social networks are bursting with data for the above two research approaches. They have the further useful characteristic of enabling the analyst to get out of his study into real social fieldwork without suffering the usual associated stresses and strains. As traditionally practised, investigations in the field raise endless problems: the selection of representative groups, elimination of obstructions and "noise", correct formulation of questions, optimisation of data collection costs, and so on. In a collaborative system much of this is no problem at all.

The social sciences peer into the future by extrapolating from the past. Ideas about tomorrow are projections from reconstructed histories, motivations and institutions of yesterday. A different approach tries to establish people's current attitude to something and attempt a forecast on that basis. Both paths are imperfect, as marketologists bringing new products on to the market know, and as those who commissioned their research know even better and to their cost. It is futile to survey putative consumers as to whether they will like some as yet unknown ware and what it should be like to make them like it. How would people have reacted to someone who forecast the popularity of Tamagotchi virtual pets or ringtones? Novelties wow the world without needing any pre-existing demand.

The methods of social prediction currently in use have more than a few shortcomings. Interviewees fantasise about what they might want if they were subject to no limitations and could ignore the cost of their answer. Some of the sharp corners can be avoided or smoothed over if the fieldwork is meticulously prepared, although few people actually have the energy to do this. With the traditional approach, however, there always remains an insuperable obstacle: a person interviewed individually or in a group is not the same person as he will be when acting in a real human environment. The circumstances in which they are talking to the interviewer have little in common with those in which they will act in the future. The main thing missing when answers are gathered by interview is that only as matters progress does it become clear what the group norm is going to be, how actions are going to fit with social pressures and social acceptability. Real-life behaviour takes its cue from leaders and trends and the attitude of people from one's own circle towards them. This dimension cannot be modelled in a research laboratory. An individual or small-group based result when projected on to the actual behaviour of large numbers of people can have an unanticipated margin of error sufficient to change a plus to a minus. This is the Achilles' heel of all experiments conducted with conveniently available human resources, whether the students of a particular professor or a different cohort. The effect is quietly passed over, but deprives the results of the greater part of their credibility. Results obtainable from a small group are not representative because of the group and network effect. They may differ startlingly from the behaviour of a large community because social solidarity has a decisive effect on the dissemination and perception of information, providing an external source of motivation. Ignoring this in experiments is tantamount to researching a tornado in a glass of water.

It is not that in large-scale social networks on the internet this very basic problem can be avoided: it simply does not and cannot exist. Collective action can be investigated there in its vast natural dimensions, not crammed into laboratory conditions. The experimental world merges with the practical world, something one could only dream of in the past.

Let us move on from these generalising remarks about methodology to examples of research which can be conducted within social networks, and let us begin with an instance which clearly shows up the limitations of traditional methods.

3.2 (Un)Happiness Economics

A serious hindrance for economic policy and economics generally is the lack of relevance of data collected by traditional methods. This is particularly noticeable when, for example, there is a need to correlate the state's economic strategy with how people are going to feel after it has been implemented. Governments do not control the quality of life either completely or directly. They can only bring about improvements in certain aspects, but which are the right economic goals and which are wrong? Which goals will citizens be grateful to see achieved? Economists need to set the overall direction of economic development so as to increase the perceived quality of life. They also need criteria to enable them to track how effective the political line chosen is proving, and to make comparisons between different countries.

On the level of common sense and common parlance, outlining the ideal towards which we should be striving might not seem all that difficult, but in fact devising workable criteria proves exceptionally difficult. The traditional approach is to identify the most important components of living: the basics, like food, accommodation, heating, clothing; then socio-cultural and educational standards; medical care; and the appropriate level of political and economic freedom. A system of quality indicators is then elaborated for each group. Most widely used is the Human Development Index (HDI) which brings together the features of life expectancy, quality of education and real GDP per capita of the population. Whether using the HDI's methodology or any other there are difficulties in devising a unitary indicator making it possible to synthesise fundamentally different features and to reflect real life convincingly. A first stumbling block becomes apparent with the effort to decide what to include in the system of indicators, and what to leave out as being too difficult to quantify. These are very evident in the educational and cultural parameters. If income and life expectancy can be calculated fairly accurately, there is no simple solution for assessing quality of education or religious freedom. Even if we could measure everything agreed to be appropriate, how are the heterogeneous parameters and logics to be reduced to a final index. Estimating the appropriate weighting is the next greasy pole. When at last, despite all these difficulties, we have a system, admittedly burdened with compromises, a final problem arises as to how to deal with the heterogeneous distribution of goods between people.

Economists and politicians have average values at their disposal, but how are they to be interpreted if that quantity of goods is not available to a majority of the population? The HDI has been published since 1990 and, despite its shortcomings, is regarded as a useful checklist. In practice, however, discussion is usually restricted to the more workable index of Gross National Product per head of the population. In other words, the conclusion is that the more goods and services there are in circulation, the better.

Right, then: economists judge a country's development on the basis of Gross National Income (GNI), the Human Development Index, or some other complex of measurable indicators. We need to understand that all these methodologies work better where there is a long way to go before basic needs are satisfied, that is, in poor countries, since many aspects of life there are closely linked to Gross National Income. As regards the "Very High Human Development" states (in the HDI rating these are the top several dozen countries), the weighted indicators balanced there are clearly unsatisfactory because the existential pulse of the society is overlooked. It can be that, despite thoroughly enviable ratings, people feel awful (as we can see, for example, from the decadent mood showing through the cosmetic mask of feature movies). To try to equate rank in the HDI ratings with how a country's citizens feel is the equivalent of judging a play's quality by the amount of scenery and stage props it has.

We can try to deduce the quality of life from the indices, but alternatively we can directly measure subjective satisfaction with life and see how closely it matches the indices. This is a way of checking the efficacy of the indices and making adjustments to them. Indicators are of value only to the extent that they help us to make people happier, which is what happiness economics attempts to do. This is a subdivision of economics which since the 1970s has been studying the correlation between objective indicators and how people actually feel. Respondents are asked directly whether they are satisfied with their life or not. The questionnaire data suggest that a sense of well-being is linked less closely to economic indicators than is commonly believed. This seems particularly to apply once a tolerable standard of living has been achieved. In different countries this ranges from US$200 to $1,200 per person per month. Below this level an increase in income has a clear positive impact on satisfaction, mainly because of a decrease in the sense of unhappiness which arises from feeling defenceless and oppressed by living in straitened circumstances. Above this level the satisfaction curve all but ceases to rise. This chimes in with data obtained from the sociology of labour and, in particular, with research into the motivation of managers. At first material recompense stimulates people to throw themselves into their work, but this stops when a certain income level is reached. It does, admittedly, restart much further up the scale, but only at very high bonus levels. In other words, although people believe that the more money a person has the better, that "better" may not be so significant as to justify the additional effort needed to earn it. If people are not hungry and already have communications facilities, then being provided with more tinned tomatoes or telecommunications will not make them much happier. This suggests that the picture obtained from lists based on economic parameters may differ from what people are actually feeling as greatly as a snapshot taken in a photo booth differs from a photographic portrait.

Although this assertion seems very obvious, actual economic policy ignores it. It carries on as if there were no lack of correlation between what it achieves and what people perceive. Intuition suggests, however, that the gap may be very wide indeed and that consequently this is an issue requiring to be studied. If our suspicions are correct, there is a need to amend both the indicators and the policy.

Numerous surveys have shown that an increase in income cannot be directly converted into an increase in happiness. There are a whole variety of reasons for this, of which the most obvious is that what matters to a person is not the absolute level of goods they possess, but that the level should be rising. The process of improvement rejoices the heart almost more than the result. People become accustomed to the level of well-being they have achieved and begin to regard it as no more than their due. They need to see improvement, but the better the situation they find themselves in the more difficult it is to achieve perceptible improvement. Gossen's law of the diminishing marginal utility of goods partly applies also to a complex of goods. It is to the merit of economists that this is taken into account when calculating HDI. A result is that people feel they are stagnating. They don't feel good. This is why it is no bad thing for the process to proceed smoothly and for improvements to take place over an extended period. Contentment is thereby prolonged.

A second, more subtle, consideration is that if we represent the correlation between contentment and objective improvements with a graph, the curve will resemble a flower petal leaning to one side. In science this form is called a hysteresis loop. Upward movement along this curve is delayed, while downward movement is accelerated. If there are swings of well-being upwards or downwards, the positive or negative part of the amplitude by which the emotions swing do not coincide. In other words, losses make people comparatively sadder than analogous gains make them happy. It is preferable for the rise to be steady and without fluctuation, even if that means there are no great leaps forward. If there are dips, there will be net emotional losses in the hysteresis.

This emotional asymmetry in perceiving life's ups and downs has a consequence which is not immediately obvious. Since there are many parameters of quality of life and not all of them will be rising at the same time, a hitch anywhere may subjectively outweigh all the gains, even if they have been achieved on many fronts. The system of weighted indicators takes no account of this, but it should. Recalculating these "downs" to their true weight can radically alter the picture.

To be completely accurate, we should also mention that events which occur less frequently evoke a hypertrophic emotional reaction. A kind of trigger operates which scales emotions up or down depending on how frequently they occur. For relatively well endowed societies success is the norm and unpleasantness is relatively rare. This means that success evokes a modest positive reaction while unpleasantness produces a sharply negative one. Those living in certain poor countries demonstrate the opposite. Their governments find it relatively easy to make their subjects, whose lives are hard, happy by tossing them a crust from time to time. People get inured to misfortune. They react less sensitively to what is just the latest disaster. At the same time they are pleased by small things. Mechanisms of emotional adjustment kick in which mitigate inequality in standards of living, blunting or sharpening perception of more frequent or rarer occurrences. The psychological metabolism of the individual and the society maintain a stable proportion of the positive and the negative and it is quite difficult to produce a relative shift from a level which has become established. We might even half seriously propose a law of conservation of happiness analogous to the law of conservation of energy. Empirical data is presented in Appendix 1 in support of this.

Mechanisms of emotional asymmetry benefit the poor and from this a number of conclusions follow in respect of policy aiming to overcome inequality. Giving priority to the initial phase of gains will target that sharply rising part of the satisfaction curve where the first small results give a marked increase in the feeling of good fortune. There should really be an area of happiness economics called unhappiness economics or, more precisely, "anti-unhappiness economics", to teach us how to climb out of unhappiness. Let those who are protected from major disasters worry about happiness. The more so since the surveys show how difficult it is to get happiness right. You can't just turn on a tap.

Interesting effects apply also to the well-off. Gossen's law of decreasing marginal utility of goods, including a totality of goods, operates as a brake on happiness, but where a complex of goods is concerned it is only partly applicable. Decreasing levels of satisfaction are obtained from collections of goods where their overall consumption does not produce a cumulative effect, but collections can be assembled in which there is a far greater increase in value than arises from each constituent in isolation. This applies to socio-functional consumption like education and creativity, or when a transition to a higher quality is ripening and needs only a little more to make it happen. Then, despite Gossen's law, an anomalous upsurge of satisfaction is observable. This rule, together with emotional hysteresis, modifies the happiness curve. It normally levels off, but here the graph looks different. Upon achieving a certain level of economic prosperity the indicators can soar upwards. This cumulative increase of value is exceptionally important in the New Economy. Traditional economics, both in theory and in practice, has a blind spot here, with the result that to date it has rarely been used effectively.

A further known cause for a discrepancy between indicators of quality of life and the individual's sense of well-being is comparison with those around you, your immediate circle. If GDP is rising, it is doing so for almost everybody at the same time with the result that there is an insufficient change in a particular individual's rating in comparison with his neighbours to generate a surge of positive emotion. By extension, a comparator which is remote in time or space is felt less keenly (except for comparison with our own youth, with all the accompanying embellishments of memory). On the whole, comparison with flourishing Danes or impoverished Papuans does not have much effect on how Russians feel (except perhaps about the glories of European socialism as depicted in the media, which we might find less palatable in reality.)

Summary indices, then, are far from summarising everything they should. There can be minuses left outside the brackets which are capable of cancelling the observed pluses. These include such things as work-related stress, anxiety about the future, the breakdown of family values, the loneliness of the big city, and culturally inspired problems with ageing and appearance. The reverse is also possible, where minuses are taken into account but not the pluses. A country may be a world leader, for example, in devising laws and standards to regulate complex, ambiguous issues like cloning, euthanasia, chemical stimulation of the brain, gay marriage, the treatment of domestic animals, problems of copyright, and receive no credit in the index for experiments which the whole world follows with interest.

The system of indicators appears to give no credit to North Americans for their unparalleled legal constructs regulating sexual harassment, consumers' rights, or the protection of children. It may be far in the future before this receives its deserved recognition. There are whole areas which have a marked effect on happiness but where objective indicators, including financial indicators, are sure to work badly. These include culture in the broad sense and cultural consumption in a narrow sense.

Although happiness economics operates with information obtained directly from people, and in consequence puts itself forward as almost a Supreme Court in respect of indices, its own methodology is not beyond reproach. There are difficulties in defining the moment in time for which the survey results can be considered valid. Obviously there can be delayed effects not evident at the time of the research, so that the results can never be regarded as final. Intensive economic growth, which inclines people to rate positively, goes hand in hand with emotional exhaustion and underinvestment in cultural capital. Everybody is pursuing money, but without a proportionate increase in symbolic capital the higher degrees of satisfaction will not be attained. Rapid growth additionally takes a bite out of the next generation's quota of happiness by pushing up the bar of expectations and engendering a dangerous split between the ideal and reality, between what young people aspire to and what they can realistically hope for. Children suffer the consequences of a misconceived parental sense of duty which aims to create favourable conditions for them but simultaneously eats away at the potential for them to enjoy achievements of their own. It is no longer the case that "children are where nature takes its holidays". Instead children take their holidays in accordance with human nature, and the older generation by allowing them to live with everything provided deprives them of the incentive to be energetic. The trajectory of a prosperous society is often likened to going up a staircase which leads downwards. That is not mere words, although it might be more accurate to liken it to trying to run up the down escalator. The pace achievable by the fittest and most successful members of society may be beyond the reach of the majority. Meanwhile the leading social groupings, maintaining their distance from the rest, shielding themselves from a sense of stagnation, continue like meths addicts to rush to new highs. But for them, as for all the others, this leads to a psychological overloading which can cancel out everything that has been achieved, as is signalled by the highly developed industry of psychotherapy. Every dollar it earns should be multiplied by 100 (if not by 1,000) and deducted from the measure of GDP.

Economics cannot really be reproached for failing to increase happiness, since the area it is responsible for is not happiness but development. If the indices are reflecting anything, it is not happiness but the provision of conditions in which a person may discover themselves, enjoy freedom to choose and surmount their circumstances. It is the complexity, the satiety and diversity of life. That is why they are called development indices. We would have far more justification for judging the validity of indices by subjective feelings of satisfaction, as happiness economics does, if people associated happiness primarily with personal freedom, but it is only a few individuals who see things in that light. Freedom and complexity are an inseparable couple, with the result that by no means everybody is free and happy at the same time (just as not all who are unfree are unhappy).

A further compromise inevitably present in happiness surveys is caused by the difficulty people face in attempting to summarise how their life feels over a longer period of time. This is why the rating of a calendar year will be heavily dependent on whether the question is asked when the interviewee is going through a good or a bad patch. A further element of randomness finds its way into responses from the fact that the present is not a unity but structured in three-part blocks of experience which include memory of the past, the present as experienced at a given moment, and the future as it is envisaged. It is uncertain which of these elements will be selected by the introspective eye, which emotions a person will voice during the survey.

The next problem arises because it is easier to rate something if you have something to compare it with; that is, if a person can simultaneously measure several comparable acts or periods against each other. On a recommendation site the users rate movies, celebrities, hotels, mobile telephones, and much else, but there is a knack to this apparently straightforward procedure. After rating several dozen or several hundred objects you may suddenly realise that you initially gave too high a rating to something right at the beginning, which has resulted in unfairness to objects experienced later. For example, you may have impulsively awarded "10" on a 10-point scale, only to come across something better. This is why judges of aesthetic forms of sport hold back the top scores for only the most outstanding performances. Because people feel the need to rerank their impressions, they should have an opportunity to review their ratings at any time. Overall ranking with the aid of paired comparison analysis is a rational algorithmic procedure which gives good results, but does not work in the relatively infrequent happiness surveys because people in most cases have nothing to compare.

To conclude: happiness surveys are not entirely harmless. Having once given voice to his rating, a person will start believing what he has said. It becomes a fact of his existence. It is entirely possible that the Russian habit of denigrating all things Russian is a reaction to an alarmingly low position in ratings. For all their drawbacks, happiness surveys are undoubtedly useful, but no matter how far their results diverge from and discredit traditional indices, economic policy will continue to be based on the latter. Governments, as indeed their peoples, tend to press on regardless in order not to look worse than others, even though it might only be necessary to re-adjust the measurement procedures to make life in a number of countries seem not to be all that dismal at all. The problem all along may just have been that those states were competing under rules ill-suited to them. It is much like entering a long distance runner in a sprint and then disparaging his performance. When they find themselves in a similar position, nations may engage in excessive self-excoriation, develop inferiority complexes and even follow someone else's path, when in fact the problem lies in the way the scores are toted up. They should be glad to have the advantages of those who are catching up because they have a potential for improvement which the leaders may already have exhausted. No less importantly, they have the opportunity of learning from other people's mistakes and taking shortcuts. The leaders too have their problems if they allow themselves to be mesmerised by the indicators, pedal faster and faster, and finally collapse in exhaustion.

Vaulting ambition led to the world financial crisis of 2008–2009. In pursuit of raising a partly fictitious quality of life, labour resources were overstrained. Some found themselves incapable or unwilling to work more intensively in order to consume more. This revealed the Achilles' heel of the New Economy with its focus on desires. An excess of goods poured off the conveyor belt, many of which could have been dispensed with without causing any real hardship. At the first serious setback customers sobered up and the mirages which, with the assistance of marketing consultants, filled their heads vanished in an instant. It became clear that a whole range of goods were not essential for personal happiness, especially when those around were tightening their belts without evident ill effects. Many cut back on consumption, dealing a cruel blow to manufacturers who found themselves working in a very sluggish market. Initially economic agents do not know which part of the assortment should be reduced and by how much, which causes them to panic. Uncertainty about the production plan spills over into uncertainty about jobs and investment. As there is no way of knowing which new business projects will be profitable tomorrow, they don't get off the ground, while those that have are frozen. This means the capital invested in them is neutralised, while credit liabilities crush borrowers. Immense resources have been put in play to keep ahead of desires, all those third and fourth houses and cottages by the river which were going to be lived in for 1 or 2 weeks a year at most.

An economy, designed to anticipate every trend in consumption, had only to falter in one place. As soon as this became widely known, manufacturers were petrified as the new climate sent business plans into negative territory. Humanity's baggage of desires, entirely manageable only yesterday, was suddenly too heavy to carry. The balance between anticipated utility from imagined goods and the frenzied pace of work needed to pay for them no longer correlated. No conventional indices reveal disjunctions of that kind. Data from happiness surveys might have signalled that something was wrong, but even they were no help in warning where the threat was coming from.

We can expect a radical improvement in prediction if we can organise systematic measurement of satisfaction levels and adjust indicators of social well-being accordingly. This is entirely realistic, bearing in mind that collaborative social networks are literally one step away from being able to provide the primary data required. They will enable us to move from sporadic survey campaigns, with all their inaccuracies, to a workable reflection of the quality of subjective time. It is a major plus for social networks that people use them for their own purposes and have no interest in observation and prediction. They register their own consumer experience (without which they cannot obtain recommendations), and as a result create detailed reports of their feelings about life. The data is collected routinely, without requiring a special effort. A subjective picture of well-being is deduced from the ratings accumulating in the database, which is more complete and more precise than that obtained by using offline surveys. The "respondent" is not placed in an artificial situation where his judgements are slewed by the fact of the survey itself. He does not answer questions about happiness but is engaged in something quite different. He gives his ratings as routinely as he makes his purchases and is not in the least interested that, by representing the demand side, he is activating the invisible hand of the market. If, however, it turns out that the user's current ratings are mostly positive although he states in happiness surveys that overall everything is terrible, that merely signals that something is wrong with his inner scale. Either he is misinterpreting the realities of his life or he is singing from someone else's hymn sheet. Possibly, when he looks at his own ratings, he will realise that all this time he was entirely happy. What a relief!

The difficulty of detecting the substance of happiness prompts us to seek a new language capable of conveying socio-cultural dynamics. The need for this has long been felt. Let the reader not be deterred by the academic phrasing of this issue. It has a direct bearing on everyday life, since being informed, having knowledge and understanding, are synonymous with action in the New Economy. A system of measurement is needed which can detect subtle movements in society dynamically, on the whole accurately, and attached to specific times, strata and groups. We also need an adequate descriptive language to replace that jingling of the fool's bells of populism which reduces a complex system of factors to primitive dilemmas, after which everybody just tries to see who can shout loudest. The third-generation internet is an environment where there is no need to dumb down and simplify because this is where the quality of subjective time can be measured. The myriad ratings of consumer actions which accumulate in the database and behind which stands the quality of time, that is the raw material we have been seeking for multi-factor dynamic analysis. Every judgement is attached to a time, to personal data, and to a clearly defined event. Any act of consumption takes its place within a series of other actions performed by a particular person, and each rating can be analysed not in isolation but within the system of his experience of life. This manifest connectivity was effectively inaccessible to researchers, but now, with the right tools at their disposal, the humanities will be able to take the next step forward.

3.3 Measuring Happiness

Traditional economics engages mainly in a struggle against imbalance, scarcity, and inequality because these are the cause of many misfortunes. If, however, there should ever be an end to the hardship of material existence then, as Schopenhauer prophesied (and not only he), the place vacated by the battle against them will be taken over by boredom. Overcoming this anticipated misfortune is a matter for the new economy. Its fundamental concern is to engage people in something meaningful at a time when the most acute problems have been solved and interesting forms of activity are in abundant supply. Admittedly, many of them will not suit everybody. For example, not everybody has the skills to be a writer. What might a positive programme of happiness look like?

The fundamental message I would like to convey is that the ultimate function of the New Economy is to build up interpersonal communications. It is not to plot against homo sapiens, who has been transformed in recent times first into homo economicus and then, in our days, increasingly been demoted to the lowly status of homo consumerensis. Opponents of the consumer society claim that this metamorphosis is occurring at the behest of capital which requires ever greater volumes of consumption in order to sell its products. The true mission of the New Economy is to create conditions for the self-discovery of each and every one of us. This can be achieved by constructing and servicing groups catering for a great variety of demands. Collaborative filtering facilitates both. While the New Economy concentrates mainly on providing goods for already identified groups, the collaborative system will help to bring people together in groups and then provide for them to interact. The precondition for this is collection of users' ratings or opinions, on the basis of which like-minded people can be identified and recommendations generated. Ratings are so interesting because they characterise both the consumption of products and those consuming them. These are aspects of a judgement about the quality of time a particular individual spends consuming a particular good or service. They enable us to derive indicators of happiness. We have only to summarise ratings of the time various people spend over a given period. The collaborative system is an already existing tool for measuring happiness.

No matter how one defines happiness, a correlation is clearly to be traced with positive experience of time. Without straining credibility, we can associate the two, whether happiness is accumulated piece by piece, like a mosaic, or whether it is spontaneous and all-embracing, as if a gift from above. When a person has many positively tinged intervals of time behind, in the present, and ahead in their life we can judge their lot to be a happy one. The greater the proportion of highly rated time and the less low rated time there is, the happier the person. In mathematical terms, the quantity of happiness is the integral of a person's quality time. For a number of reasons the person himself may determine this integral very inaccurately. If every fragment of life without exception could be rated, the sum of the ratings would characterise happiness perfectly. For the present, to obtain totally complete data is not an option. Indeed, it is unattainable in principle, and it is not actually needed. It is enough that, as recommender practice expands into new areas, quantitative indicators will accumulate. With time the map of subjective satisfaction will be sufficiently detailed to serve for practical purposes. In a number of respects it is already perfectly usable thanks to the millions of users of recommendation sites who systematically rate the movies and plays they have seen, books they have read, and so on. In so doing they have documented an appreciable proportion of their cultural activity and, in order to understand how it influences the sense of happiness, we have only to multiply the assessments by the length of time involved. Such calculations are not difficult, given that the duration of particular types of cultural consumption is fairly standard. For simplicity's sake, we will disregard the effects of post-experience and aftertaste. We can thus weight the proportion of cinema, theatre, music and reading. Let us suppose that over the course of a year a person has watched 200 movies and the distribution peak of the ratings he has given is "8". From this we may deduce that the cinema industry has presented him with some 300 h of, by his own criteria, extremely high quality time. If, after five theatre visits he has not once come away with impressions deserving more than a "5", which signifies "average", then he has misspent 15 h and they should be subtracted from his symbolic income. On this simple example we can see the kind of practical use which can be made of observation of ratings. Either he should stop going to the theatre, accepting that in its current state it is not to his taste, or he should take greater care about the productions he chooses (perhaps making better use of the recommender service).

The very first analysis of data extracted from ratings promises to yield new knowledge. For example, if we measure volumes of quality time and extrapolate it per head of the population in areas like cinema, literature and music as far as is currently practicable, we will be able to establish the current norm of happiness. In addition, from the ratings statistics we will be able to derive directly the distribution of personal time and money budgets between different types of leisure, and to study for each individual the conversion rates of objective time into quality time. It will also be possible to compare the financial cost of different ways of achieving the same degree of satisfaction or, from the opposite angle, to establish differences in the quality of time acquired for a particular level of expenditure. If, for example, it is made generally known that movies and shows on free access TV channels on average rate 2 points lower than those on pay services, the number of subscribers to the latter will increase. Such are some of the ways we can work with the statistical data which accumulate in a Web 3.0 system. There is more detailed discussion of this in the Appendix.

3.3.1 Measuring Subjective Time

Since we are giving so much prominence to subjective time, let us consider the concept carefully and define it as intrapersonal experience of objective time. A very important characteristic of inner time is a person's subjective estimate of how much time passed while he was engaged in something and not looking at his watch. There is a lot of evidence to indicate that perceived (psychological) time and objective (chronological) time do not necessarily coincide and that, moreover, depending on his emotional state, a person may underestimate or overestimate the length of time which has elapsed by a factor of several times. Chronological time flows evenly, so what is happening to it in the human mind? The greatest intellects have grappled with this question, beginning with St Augustine who associated inner time with a distension of the soul, and continuing with Immanuel Kant and Henri Bergson. The same interest permeates the writings of Marcel Proust, James Joyce, and others. Not only poets and thinkers, but all of us occasionally catch ourselves thinking that time is flowing anomalously and that our inner chronometer is out of sync with the hands of the clock. When you are eagerly anticipating something, time drags agonisingly slowly, and if you are engrossed in something it flies by.

There are well known experiments confirming that this inner sense of time is no illusion but an innate human ability. It is a sixth sense (or seventh if you add the sense of balance to the usual five). It is a universal characteristic and everybody's inner clock can speed up or slow down. This is particularly noticeable if there are no external signals to confirm the passage of time. Test subjects lose their sense of time if they are in caves or immersed in salt baths which deprive the sensory organs of signals. The same effects are observed in subjects under hypnosis, suffering sleep deprivation, or taking narcotic substances. At the end of the nineteenth century it was discovered in Wilhelm Wundt's laboratory that certain people systematically underestimate the duration of time while others overestimate it. It has also been observed that the perception of time is dependent on the nature of external stimuli. Visual signals of exactly the same duration appear longer than auditory ones. If a period of time is divided into short intervals, it is perceived as having been extended. Short intervals lead to overestimation and long intervals to underestimation. Such experiments are studying the basic human ability to determine duration, and test subjects need to have a balanced state of mind. Emotions are seen as flawing the experiment.

We, however, are precisely interested in the perception of time in different psychological and emotional states. Subjective time or, as it is called, psychological, inner, personal, or intrapersonal time, differs both from objective chronological time and from the time registered by our biological clocks responsible for the functioning of the vital organs. These second and third kinds of time are not considered here, and we will say nothing about social time. Depending on one's state of mind, time may be experienced as flowing smoothly or advancing in leaps and bounds, as compressed or extended, full or empty. It proceeds unevenly. It is irregular, multi-faceted and manipulable. None of these features applies to chronological time.

The fact that perceived duration of time correlates directly with the subject's psychological and emotional state and the kind of activity he is engaged in can act as the starting point for some extremely interesting research. A powerful motivation is the feeling that subjective time is somehow associated with the mysterious quality of human existence, and the hope that time might somehow be tamed. Indeed, if perception of time can vary widely, how can we contrive to extend the boundaries as much as possible? To rule time would be in some measure to surmount the finite nature of individual existence. Like all living things, human beings have an inborn aversion to death, and this is augmented by a culture which elevates the value of life to an absolute. It is not difficult to guess why culture does this, but the thought that this highest good is not bestowed in perpetuity can truly poison human existence. Other cultures had different attitudes to the matter of life and death. The culture of ancient Egypt, for example, did not present the afterlife as being particularly scary. Despite the fact that our attitude to death is dictated by nature, the human mind seems close to understanding how to mitigate or altogether do away with the fear of death.

We need to rebrand the idea of life, shifting the emphasis from the nominal to the subjective duration of time. If we can move from thinking about gross quantity to net quality the problem will be half solved. The need is to move the hands of the clock from objective time to inner time, and learn to slow them down.

This is possible because the sensation of time is directly dependent on the experiences with which it is filled. Sergey Rubinshtein formulated the "Law of the emotionally determined assessment of time". Time, filled with events with a positive emotional connotation, is experienced as condensed. When filled with events with negative emotional connotations it is extended. At first glance this looks very unpromising. What is so great about the fact that positive time flows by quickly? Indeed, if the quality of time and its duration are in inverse proportion, then what you gained by increasing one you would lose by decreasing the other and would end up with no net gain. Fortunately, quite the opposite happens. How long a life lasts subjectively depends on how it is remembered, on post-factum rating of its fullness and duration. William James, the psychologist and founder of pragmatism, said much the same as Rubinshtein: "In general, a time filled with varied and interesting experiences seems short in passing...". However, James immediately went on to perplex the reader with a paradox: "...but long as we look back. On the other hand, a tract of time empty of experiences seems long in passing, but in retrospect short". Thus, perception of duration during the process is the exact opposite of what it is after it concludes. A person engrossed in what he is doing keeps no track of time, and accordingly it flows by rapidly. When he comes to recollect it, however, it plays back in his consciousness as having lasted for ages. Similarly, if someone has spent time empty of experiences, instead of living he has merely suffered time's unbearable slowness. He has nothing to remember other than his own wretchedness. Now everything has been turned upside down: subjective duration is a function which increases in line with the quality of time. Time well spent generally impresses itself in memory as having been full and long lasting, and its contribution to the money box of life has been substantial. As we noted earlier, the integral of quality personal time can be seen as quantifying happiness. Now we can see that it simultaneously indicates subjective duration, which is closely connected with the perceived quality of time. Accordingly, maximising the integral means winning the race against the time nature has allotted us. In this light, living two or three times more intensively is tantamount to living the same amount longer and with better quality. On the other hand, to live with zero intensity is close to not living at all. In other words, in order to live a long life, we need to fill the years we have as fully as possible with experiences. This process is something anyone can manage since no abnormal sensitivity is required to recognise the interconnection between the emotional colouration of time, its intensity, and its perceived duration. Most people are capable of this, which means that if they so wish they should not find it particularly difficult to master this kind of self-regulation.

The link between time and the emotions has been confirmed many times experimentally, and also by clinical research. Manic patients greatly underestimate the duration of present time, while people in depressive states overestimate it. The experience of time differs markedly between well-adjusted and maladjusted adolescents. For the latter, the passage of time is empty and unengaging. They look to the past, not the future. The same is observed in people who are chronically stressed.

From the above we would seem to have arrived at a handy recipe for increasing the effective duration of life: we should just do all we can to fill our time and to keep our mind and soul busy. Unfortunately, this is not a practical recipe but mere wishful thinking, which it will remain unless we can devise a way of bringing the whole idea down to earth by proposing a generally accessible method. Psychology explains a lot about subjective time, but gives no instructions on how to optimise it. At this point we can turn to the concept of personal time elucidated by K.A. Abulkhanova-Slavskaya. She advises that the recipe for true longevity is to live "deeply". She talks about the "quality of personal time" and links it to self-realisation. This may sounds like a truism, adding nothing to the familiar concepts of "having a good time" and "quality of life". As soon as a person begins to track subjective time and register their attitude to it, however, the situation changes radically. The term "quality" takes on a specific meaning and practical sense. In order to advance to the management of personal time it is necessary only to distinguish gradations of quality, to document them and be guided by those standards (as yet undefined). These elements are not included in Abulkhanova–Slavskaya's concept, but her conclusion is that we need to give priority to timeliness, by which she means filling time in the best way possible in the given circumstances. (Let us note that this wish is formulated in full accordance with economic logic.) The problem is that it is no easier to define a measure of timeliness than to define the parameters of quality. Merely replacing one clarion call with another will not move us forward. A separate issue is indicators of human time: they need to be simple and to fit readily into everyday routine. What is the point of characteristics which can only be measured in a specially equipped laboratory? Of course, neither is it any use proposing indicators unless we can persuade people to use them.

In a word, what is needed is regular rating of the quality of subjective time and an easy way of registering the results. Happily, neither of these is impossible. It is as natural for a person to register the quality of time as to breathe. It is an innate (and trainable) ability, as is indicated by the millions of ratings in various collaborative systems. The procedure does not require any special effort on the part of participants, nothing beyond what they are already accustomed to doing on the site when they post ratings. Let us not forget that by quality of time we have in mind a generalised emotional distillate of everything that fills time: experiences, reflections, insights, calculations, meditations, creativity. This characterisation is unnuanced and conveys only the vividness of an emotional colouration, positive or negative.

How differentiated should the scale of measurement of quality time be? In theory it should, on the one hand, correspond to people's ability to distinguish gradations of quality, and on the other provide an optimal balance between the intensiveness and precision of computer calculations. From the experience of recommendation sites, a five-point scale is not really sufficient. A ten-point scale is (and in the specialist literature one will find arguments in favour of a seven-point scale). If it is to become a tool for personal self-management, the rating of inner time should become a habit and occur almost unthinkingly. A good way of achieving this is by combining it with some routine activity, and here there is nothing better than the third-generation social networks where reflecting on the quality of time dovetails nicely with satisfying a whole range of other needs, such as navigation, self-presentation and socialising. It remains only to recognise this and start making ratings. Accordingly, to master the practice of managing subjective time it is necessary to: (1) make it a rule to rate the quality of personal time; (2) register the results in numerical form.

Although some of what is said here about subjective time is a matter for the future, managing it is not something unprecedented. Each of us is conscious to a greater or lesser degree of the potential value of our time, and to the best of our abilities we maximise the return from it. Everybody has a different planning horizon, with some people maximising their pleasures within the limits of the next half hour while for others it is decades. Some forms of activity are accepted as mutually complementing each other, with neither having to be given priority. Undemanding reading matter admirably complements the pleasures of the beach, while an intellectual who has worked hard need not be ashamed of preferring a low-brow movie to a profound and serious masterpiece, simply because at that particular moment he does not have the emotional resources to engage with the masterpiece. Having a rational attitude towards time does not mean squeezing the maximum out of every moment. That is just as prodigal as running full tilt in a long distance race. It is also fairly obvious that in the longer term the optimum will be to maintain a balance between activity creating the preconditions for future quality time and activity which gives an immediate return. Certain occupations are on the borderline, for example, gaining knowledge and, more broadly, consuming information. There is an obvious parallel with the way factories maintain a balance between preparation and actual production. When allocating time to various types of activity it will make sense to build up a balanced portfolio the way investors do. This should include "growth stocks" so that, when earlier activities begin to bore you, you have something to switch to. To conclude this list of helpful advice from the author on how to live your life, do retain a sense of moderation and do not get caught in a treadmill of time optimisation so that agonising about that does not mar the time it is supposed to improve. There are other fairly straightforward techniques for time management, but for most people they would not be acted on until a clear, systematic method has been devised.

The category of quality time allows us to understand a number of phenomena which are otherwise difficult to explain. Many people are puzzled when they observe notably carefree people totally devoting themselves to business. If we put to one side the suspicion that their supposedly Herculean overworking is a myth, their improbable busyness really does look to an outsider like Aristotle's chrematistics, that is, making money for the sake of making money. In reality however, as we can now understand, for certain types of personality this is a way of maximising the quality of time. The position of the head of the firm, apart from its obvious material rewards, gives scope for freely managing time and personal resources. The leader himself determines the pace of work and play. He chooses when, with whom, and under what circumstances he will resolve particular issues; which of his pet schemes he will realise in practice; and what degree of dependence on the will of other players he is prepared to tolerate. If a person is possessed by a desire to organise his world so that within its confines everything should operate in accordance with the rules he establishes, no amount of prosperity will persuade him to stop.

A capitalist who has become an addict of this kind of motivation is disinclined to allocate more than a modest percentage of his income to personal consumption. All the rest is ploughed back into his business and, in most cases, serves to benefit society. This is the moral justification of capitalism and altogether a strong argument in favour of it which seems never to have been clearly expressed. It seemed sufficient to claim that free capitalist competition between individuals pursuing egotistical aims works for the benefit of society as a whole. In fact, however, the benefit derives not so much from competition as from the fact that it goads the capitalist into reinvesting income in the business. De jure, the capital belongs to a private individual, but de facto that individual is stewarding it on behalf of the other members of society. Whether people are aware of the fact or not, entrepreneurs slog away not merely for their own benefit, but for the good of society.

The capitalist system concentrates capital and resources in the hands of those most capable of managing them. What the capitalist maximises is not money for his personal consumption (as far as that goes, the margin of utility is soon reached), but the opportunity to be his own master and the quality of personal time, a condition of which is the economic power he has acquired. Freedom for self-realisation and the scope for large-scale risk-taking are goods of which people never tire. As regards material freedom and physiological comfort, these, like any utilitarian goods which have become habitual, are perceived as no more than what is due. The least encroachment on them, however, will produce a sharply negative reaction and oblige the capitalist, regardless of his overworking, to rush to the defence of the status quo.

Managers one step down are already restricted in respect of this kind of freedom and beholden not only to circumstances but also to the management above them. They give up part of their freedom in return for guarantees and support from above. Those at the base of the pyramid of hired labour usually have very little freedom, but that does not deprive them of opportunities for self-realisation in their profession. It follows from this, inter alia, that Nietzsche's notorious Will to Power, which has generated so much philosophical discussion and raised such a hullabaloo in Russian society, is merely a particular instance of a strategy aimed at acquiring quality time. This demystifies this human characteristic. In no way is it an inborn trait of human nature, as a familiar doctrine insists. The will to power is explicable as an aspiration to personal freedom, to be able to occupy yourself as you please, when and with whom you please. Power over others is a means of enabling a person to regulate relations between himself and his inner time. It is not the will to power but the quality of time to which everything can be traced back. These are the terms in which it should ultimately be interpreted. The primal principle on which any society is organised is the erection of a vertical hierarchy, and this too is associated with people's aspiration to control time. To some degree that is why they climb the social ladder in the first place, in order to be able to impose on those below them the calendar they personally desire.

Recognising that inner time can be both positive and negative enables us to clarify a number of issues, the better to understand the processes of the New Economy. Choice, as we have seen, comes at a price. When that was realised, an amendment was made to the idea of classical economics that man was an ideal maximiser. It was seen that, when choosing, a person will eventually finds it makes better sense to stop at a satisfactory option rather than go on seeking the absolute best, as there is no guarantee that the additional search costs will be recouped. As Simon put it, the search continues until the additional marginal costs outweigh the anticipated gain from the search. This notion can be further refined by adding that we need to take account not only of time and psychological costs, but also of the value of the time spent in choosing.

That process may itself give pleasure, and then the costs should be reduced by that amount and the search continued for longer than would be appropriate if it were not the case. On the other hand, the search may be exhausting and disagreeable, and then it would make sense to reduce the search time. The desire to avoid negative time spent on searching and anticipation means we need to be less picky. It is on this attitude that markets in which information is not transparent, including the cultural markets, often prey. The consumer agrees to practically the first thing he is offered, just in order to terminate disagreeable search time as quickly as possible. The burden of negative time spent choosing pulls down the average level of the quality of time lived.

3.3.2 Research into Emotional Dynamics

Subjective time is associated with the emotions, and these have been little better studied than time itself. It would be good to have a clear picture at our disposal of the development of emotions, but for the time being we have to make do with very general, mostly artistic, representations. If the absence of knowledge about subjective time can be explained by its being overshadowed by time in general, emotions, on the contrary, are in full view. The preparatory work has already been done by psychologists. Theories have been proposed, emotions classified. It would be good now to embark on detailed study of their dynamics, to see how one succeeds another, how they unite and form stable combinations. Research in this area would have a clear practical application. When we are talking about happiness, itself regarded as an emotion, the role of emotions in a person's inner life is clearly very important. In the near future we can expect to see the emergence of markets and of technologies associated with the management of emotions. So far, though, as in the study of other dynamic processes, the social sciences have had little success.

Even without research we can state with confidence that every emotion has a beginning, an end and a characteristic duration (which will be different for different emotions). We know, for example, that the acute phase of grief following bereavement lasts around 6 months (Vitis Vilyunas). As regards other emotions, we have only a modicum of knowledge about how they develop, and in particular about their duration. We may surmise that for each personality type a particular order and range of emotions is desirable, and that departures from this ideal will have consequences. A person needs to undergo certain experiences at particular times, but circumstances sometimes prevent this and cause a strong, often unrecognised and unsatisfied demand for situations which would enable harmonious emotional states to develop. If there is a shortage of certain experiences, a person's emotional life may be disfigured, deviate from what is optimal, and be in need of correction. The individual tries his best to overcome the deficiency by seeking or even unconsciously setting up situations to provide an outlet for his emotions. Long suppressed irritation, for example, may burst out entirely inappropriately over some trifling matter.

At this point it is worth turning our attention to one of the most pleasing but neglected attributes of art and the entire realm of the aesthetic. Art is a universal means of regularising the emotions. Aesthetic culture is a factory which manufactures experiences. Its storerooms are bursting with emotions preserved in texts, images and sounds (as well, of course, as with plenty of stuff which is past its sell-by date or was never much good in the first place.) Delving into these storerooms, a person can live a kind of other life which suffuses and expands his own. At the same time he enhances his emotional repertoire and learns to empathise: he sorts out his own "emotiogram". These storerooms have the very valuable characteristic of being freely accessible, enabling a person to take advantage of them at a time to suit himself. From this point of view the very existence of culture assumes special significance.

As with subjective time, collaborative practice also has a role in the studying of emotions. This would require a facility for registering emotions when rating works or other objects. On a software level this is not difficult. Some people will rush to see it as a further step towards mechanisation of the soul, the pharmacy issuing emotions on prescription (or without). I see no genuine threat here, especially since the idea is unlikely ever to be fully implemented. This upgrade to the cultural supermarket might even be welcome. What is wrong with delivering works in the light of demand for particular emotions? A similar service has been provided for years by music sites which will select music for a particular mood, and so far there have been no fatalities.

Although in the present volume inner time and emotional dynamics are considered only as they relate to collaborative practice, research in these areas obviously cannot be so restricted. Other approaches will need to be brought in, among them computer-assisted linguistics (semantic analysis of the blogosphere), computer-assisted tomography, neurobiology, research into sleep and dreams. A special place in this research should be reserved for music, which is based on perception of durations and is, of all the arts, the one most closely associated with subjective time.

3.4 The Measure of Symbolic Exchange: Second Money

Having introduced the concept of subjective time we can now move on to the already mentioned matter of a measure for the symbolic. Until now this fundamental problem has unavoidably been put to one side, but all other attempts to devise a system of measurement in the humanities tie in with it. What is this measure? How, for example, is the value of a blockbuster to be compared with that of an art movie? Such traditional indicators as star ratings and box-office takings are, as we have seen, pseudo-measures of symbolic value. They are more likely to mislead than to enlighten. Who cares if some smash hit watched by millions has pulled in ten times more time and money than a movie with an audience of 100,000? We simply do not know the cultural impact of either of them, emotional, social, educational, developmental or other. Quite possibly that matters more than the difference in the size of their audiences. But then again, perhaps it doesn't. Within one system of coordinates art movies are more valuable, within another blockbusters are. No matter what may be said, no agreement will be possible before we start using the concept of the quality of inner time.

A work of art's impact is determined by the quantity of associated quality time, which theoretically depends on the number of moviegoers (recipients), their level of cultural capital, and the strength of the impression made on each of them. Alas, the two latter quantities are completely unknown. Even points ratings indicating the degree of satisfaction do not help much because they do not contain the information needed to enable us to correctly correlate, for example, 100,000 viewings at an average rating of "6" with 10,000 ratings at an average of "9". Bearing in mind that the starting point for a positive reaction is "5" (the so-called semantic zero in the 10-point scale), and taking account of how far ratings deviate from it in either direction, it would seem possible to even out the difference in the numbers of ratings. Alas, this approach, despite its obvious arithmetical neatness, gets us nowhere. The problem is that we do not know what psychological distance separates a "9" from a "6". The points on the scale denoting the force of the impression made are not equidistant. For example, the jump from "7" to "8" may correspond in subjective perception to an increase two times, even three times, greater than a rise from "6" to "7". We do not know. We can only say that if we had data about the true state of affairs, we would obtain a steeply rising curve, but exactly how steep we cannot say. There is no certainty either that gradations of satisfaction are identical in different sectors of consumption. It is logical to suppose that they differ. In short, the points from a satisfaction curve are turned into a logarithmic scale, and we can say nothing more definite than that. It seems reasonable to ask whether people would prefer five "7" movies or one with a "10" rating, but for a number of reasons it is quite impossible to establish this, and even direct questioning is unlikely to shed any light. From the statistics accumulated by recommendation sites we can see that there are between two and nine "8"s for every "9". Given that range of dispersal it is impossible to establish a norm. The only thing that is clear is that this correlation is associated in some way with the short supply of high-quality movies, and that cinemagoers are unable to find them when they want them. It also seems to indicate that people need something light and relaxing, something to pass the time, and that plays into the hands of "7"-rated movies.

Our example is taken from the cinema, but it would not be difficult to find any number of other illustrations of the limited reliability of points. For example, it would be absurd to compare the points awarded to a joke, a video blog, or a ringtone with ratings of major art forms. We are dealing here with categories of entirely different weight. Points are uninformative not only when comparing different kinds and genres of art. For example, some reasonably well edited entertainment movie will have little trouble earning itself an "8" in the context of similar products with no particular pretensions. That same "8" will be awarded to an outstanding movie which has won it in the heavyweight category of major art. Obviously, these are "8"s of differing magnitude, but the points system blurs the difference. Despite the fact that ratings do not reflect an absolute value, they are better than nothing. In many cases, where all that is needed is a straightforward hierarchy, the points system works reasonably well. It works, for example, for collaborative filtering or in the awarding of examination marks in the education system. It is incapable, however, of producing absolute measurements.

If we can't use ratings, box-office takings, or points, what can we use as a measure of symbolic value? The fact of the matter is that right now there is nothing suitable. However, the fact that we don't currently have a measure does not mean that one could not be created. The measure of the symbolic could be gratuity payments, that is, ordinary money used in the extraordinary function of post factum voluntary payments. The more donations an item collects, the higher its value. As this method of expressing satisfaction through monetary supplements becomes the norm, so values will be given numerical expression and it will be possible to rank them in order of the amount of money they attract.

The logic behind this solution is that symbolic value (applied to works) or symbolic capital (applied to artists) become visible through their ability to engender quality time. The measure of this ability can be gratuity money, as that is what reveals the subjective attitude of recipients to value. The fact that post factum payment (which is crucial if measurement is to be possible) is relatively rare at present should not put us off. This is learned behaviour. There are many signs that donating money is becoming normal and likely to grow in the near future. In the first place, a kindred phenomenon is already showing a considerable head of steam, in that education, medicine and the protection of nature, for example, are largely financed privately by charitable donations, and indeed the purchase of branded goods at thrice the price is itself not far removed from covert voluntary donation. In the second place, we know that in the past culture existed largely on the basis of patronage. It seems entirely natural to re-introduce this model, at least in part, in the latest spiral of history, with the difference that major donations will be replaced or supplemented by popular micro-patronage on a massive scale. Supplementary payments have an entirely utilitarian motivation, which also stimulates both producers and users. If we free ourselves of the prejudice against the "mercenariness" of money, it is easy to see how close a gratuity scheme is to the spirit of human relationships.

Now that we have a claimant to the role of a measure of value, let us support it by showing how the measurement might work in practice. At the same time, we will see that it is the only approach possible.

It is generally accepted that the only way of measuring the value of goods is in relation to other goods. It cannot be inferred a priori and becomes visible only in exchange, with each side pursuing its own advantage and unwilling to give more for the good than it is judged to be worth. But what if products are not directly bartered for each other? If there is a good which participates in all exchanges, value can be expressed in units of that good, and in practice it is money which is the good universally exchanged. In the symbolic field, however, money is a bad instrument of measurement because it does not have stable purchasing power. An incontrovertible sign of money's failure in this realm is uniform prices for entirely different digital products. Books, movies and sound recordings all cost the same, irrespective of their content or quality. For the symbolic we need some analogue of money, but one which corresponds to its needs and specifics. We need first to establish what the features of this second money should be, and then we will see how to arrive at it. Let us first think about the standard market measures of cost. What are the qualities of exchanged objects and what are the procedures which make quantitative evaluation possible? Knowledge of the inner workings of this mechanism will help us to discover second money.

In the first place, to measure value we can use only something which is itself a limited resource. At least, it should be in short supply with the parties to the exchange, since otherwise the claimant to the role of the means of measurement would be exchanged for a needed good in arbitrary amounts, and would reveal neither the true need for the product nor serve as a measure of its value. A person has no shortage of rating points (except in rare situations where they are artificially limited), and accordingly points cannot serve as an instrument of measurement. In the second place, although value does exist in human minds, it is no easy matter to extract it from there. Even the individual himself will have difficulty estimating in purely intellectual terms how precious a particular object is to him, and to give a number to that value. He needs guidelines for comparison. In just the same way, it is difficult to gain a sense of the intensity of human sensations, experiences and motivations until they become manifest in decisions and actions. Value becomes objectivised in exchange and in no other way. Its primary indicator is the human individual, a kind of testing probe. Guided by his feelings, a person decides what quantity of a good in short supply (money) he is prepared to part with in exchange for a particular value. This decision cannot be taken in isolation, independently of other deals, and without their all taking their place within the context of the budget at the individual's disposal. People can feel their way towards the monetary equivalent of value only through the regular practice of allocating their budget to categories of essential expenditure. Hence the third, least recognised but no less important, condition of the functioning of the traditional monetary system is the uniformity or repetitiveness of deals. In order to allocate the budget knowledgeably, the individual needs to have an idea of the value of particular goods, and for this he needs first to have experienced them. In addition, it is desirable to be able to estimate how well the selection of goods complement each other. Underlying more or less firm prices is the repetitiveness of acts of consumption. Providing there is uniformity and openness of dealings, the market mechanism of supply and demand reduces numerous private, subjective assessments to single prices. That is, it produces intersubjectivity of assessment. Quite soon an average ("fair") price emerges which serves as a guideline for the parties. In the absence of repetitiveness and openness, for example when a good is constantly changing or deals are done in secret, the market is incapable of measuring value. If it does, there will be a wide margin of error.

Let us analyse symbolic exchange in the light of the three preconditions for monetary measurement listed above. Their presence will indicate where we can simply follow the logic of ordinary money, but their absence will oblige us to consider modifications.

At least we do have one essential element, and that is a subject capable of judging value. Things are less easy in respect of everything else. As we have said, goods bearing value which is to be measurable by the market must be scarce, and the subjective need for them derives from past experience. The symbolic does not have this quality of scarcity. It is released into the air, it is on open access: on the internet, in libraries, in the ether and, with few exceptions, it is as free as air. (The exceptions include anything which has a material shell which is difficult to reproduce, for example theatre and graphic art.) This of itself virtually rules out monetary measurement. Unlike material goods and services, the consumption of symbolic products by one person does not deprive others of the same opportunity. Indeed, it is often case that the more extensive the circle of consumers, the better. The product may be present in unlimited quantities and is not removed from subsequent consumption, so where is its scarcity? One can artificially bar access and then demand payment to restore it, but given today's facilities for copying and distributing content that is already almost impossible and likely to be even more problematical in the future (unless the content producers manage to lobby through wholly draconian measures against private individuals who infringe copyright). Symbolic products are not competitive and cannot be excluded from consumption. This is symptomatic of social goods which do not have to be paid for and which accordingly are at the mercy of freeloaders. Since symbolic exchange does not require strict observation of parity of benefit to the parties, the motive to track the proportions of the exchange disappears, with the result that no measurements are made. Conventional exchange reveals value precisely through the mechanism of firm recompense.

Let us abandon the dead end approach through scarcity of the symbolic product and try a different angle. Let us seek what could theoretically serve as an instrument of measurement in the symbolic realm. Clearly this should be universal and also in limited supply, since otherwise we will find ourselves trying to use a ruler with a movable scale. Perhaps time will serve? It seems a logical partner for the symbolic, no worse than money for the material. Time is plainly a limited resource and people have a fair idea of its value. Consumption of the symbolic involves the spending of time, and it should be possible to judge the value of particular products from the quota of time allocated to them. Alas, the idea of using time as an instrument of measurement does not survive closer scrutiny.

If the anticipated utility of each cultural good was based on experience, then allocating part of the budget of time to it might possibly tell us about its value. The newer an information product is, however, the less predictable is its effect, and the more predictable it is, the less is its effect. The undoubted fact that the non-repetitive nature of symbolic goods hinders calibration of value using time is only half the problem. Time has another fundamental defect which puts an end to its candidacy. Of the two requirements a measure of value must meet, that it should: (a) be limited and (b) a valuable resource, time meets only the first. It is always limited, but by no means always valuable. The inner psychological value of periods of time of equal duration is highly variable. The real snag about measuring by the hour is that willingness to spend time very much depends on the value of what is laying claim to it. Lacking a stable value, time lacks the consistent purchasing power characteristic of money.

Worse is to come. Time nullifies its purchasing ability every second, urging a person to use it without delay and irrespective of the price. You cannot save it, cannot deposit it in the bank, cannot make it grow. It is spent irrespective of whether you intend to spend it or not. The impossibility of putting off the act until a more suitable moment devalues time and disqualifies it from being used to as a measure of values. If something analogous were to happen to money, that is, if it ever encountered a negative interest rate, everything in the world would change. If money burnt your hands, a person would throw it away on the first good that came along just in order to be rid of it. In such a situation there is no incentive to check parity or to weigh decisions. Information theory explains money by the need to use it to take a pause in exchange deals, giving one the opportunity to choose the optimal variant. Money mediates exchange, splitting the transfer of values from one set of hands to another into the two stages of buying and selling, and one can wait out the interval between them by using money. Time cannot function as an exchange intermediary because in the course of the exchange it will have been permanently reduced.

Accordingly, there is a void on both sides of the exchange equation. Measurement is the comparison of two scarcities, but there is none on either side of the scales. In one there is information, the value of which is to be measured but which is tending towards being a free good. On the other is the time which is spent on consumption of the information and, although in principle it is in short supply, that is not the attribute it is showing here. To correlate the one with the other is like to trying to balance two vacuums.

Labyrinthine as the maze may be, there is a way out of it, which we will find if we view symbolic exchange as a means of transforming an individual's calendar time into quality subjective time. Speaking in purely economic terms, a person should allocate to the perception of various kinds of information such quotas of time (also of attention and other personal resources) as will yield a maximum of well filled and high-quality subjective time. This is not information in general, but the subjectively valuable part of information which engenders quality personal time, and that is the scarce resource we are seeking. Optimising time means (a) to use it in a timely manner; and (b) to fill it with valuable and valued content. This can be realised if content of the requisite quality is always to hand. Then, when a window of time appears, there will be options available with which to occupy it.

Although by and large there is no shortage of content, as soon as we start talking about the part which is of personal significance to a particular consumer, the shortage becomes as acutely perceptible as information about the quality of content is meagre. The access to value is obstructed by heaps of trash which has to be shovelled aside before one can reach anything deserving of attention. Since subjectively high-quality information has scarcity, its value should become apparent in the process of discovering it. This is precisely what occurs in a collaborative system: the second money it activates, and all the rest, serves as payment for high-quality information, including data on the quality of the information itself. In accordance with the collaborative principle one may not obtain a prediction without expending resources on creating one's own profile, in the course of which the operation of subjectively weighing up value is performed which finds quantitative expression in post factum payment.

When a large number of people reveal their view of value, that is itself a process of measuring it. It is essential, however, that this should be accompanied by the expenditure of resources which belong to them. The scarcity which is a condition for measurement of value is not where you would usually find it, not on the supply side with the necessary material resources, but on the side of consumption and, accordingly, of personal resources. This process of collaborative assessment of value is in some ways analogous to what occurs in conventional markets. By making purchases, a person satisfies his basic needs and only in passing, and in most cases without realising it, participates in the measurement of value, influencing the price. In our case, a person is striving to optimise his choice as a cultural consumer and also thanking the creative artist. To do so he performs a number of actions, a side effect of which is measurement. In return he receives indispensable navigation assistance. In this way, when measuring symbolic values the same conditions are observed as in the utilitarian sphere: the process is linked to many acts of exchange; it serves to optimise consumer choice; and additionally it is an incidental but inextricable part of exchange.

The idea of measurement by means of second money can be explained in another way, by making use of the concept of "consumer surplus". This is how economists designate the difference between the sum paid in accordance with the price list and the amount a person would in principle be willing to pay if he knew in advance the utility he would obtain from his purchase. The sum of consumer surpluses, if it were published, would signal symbolic value. Although people are normally disinclined to reveal information which might be used to their disadvantage (for example, to raise prices), in the case of collaborative filtering the situation is the reverse: it is advantageous to communicate information, and this leads to personal gain.

The formula proposed in the last chapter, "time–text–time[1]", describing the transformation of time into quality personal time, develops into the series: calendar time–second money–prediction of subjective value of information (recommendations)–quality time of the individual. Let us again define what is in this chain:

calendar time: a resource rationally expended as a result of collaborative filtering;
quality subjective time: increasing this is the aim of optimising the use of calendar time;
second money: ordinary money but used in an extraordinary manner, under a system of post factum payment. It serves as a measure of symbolic value, and builds the user profile which is essential for efficient navigation and access to values. Underlying measurement are subjective opinions objectivised through voluntary payments. The latter cannot be avoided without causing damage to the user profile;
collaborative filtering: a means of rating and predicting the quality of information, and simultaneously a pledge of conscientious rating/value judgements (without which the user will be ejected from the group of recommenders).

However complex the system which conjoins collaborative filtering and second money, this is the solution to a problem which until now was considered insoluble. Moreover, everything relating to filtering has already been tried and tested. It is worth remembering that until quite recently this evoked no less scepticism than retrospective donation schemes of recompense do today. We believe that the business model of trust advertising will shortly help to overcome this scepticism, since it employs second money and is a hot topic. Without it no way can be seen of resolving the acute problem of monetising content production (as discussed in Chap. 2).

And indeed, the method described for introducing it is not that difficult, bearing in mind the extraordinary nature of the task and the fact that everybody had lost hope that any solution existed. We are hardly going to measure talent in the proposed currency of "gauguins". After extensive and fruitless searching it would be naive to expect a simple, one step solution. If there was one, it would have been found long ago. This did not occur because certain essential components of the solution were missing: post factum micro-payments and collaborative filtering. Today they have appeared, but to implement micro-patronage there is no escaping the need for major institutional changes.

[1]The measurement of subjective time by using second money affords an opportunity to calculate the results of symbolic exchange, and in particular its impact on culture. If germane methods appear in culture for measuring symbolic value, natural indicators and regulators or processes will arise which will allow symbolic markets to escape from their domination by commerce. Money for culture should not be generated artificially outside of culture and presented to it on a plate. It should emerge only from evaluation of subjective time through joint efforts. At first this will be done only through ratings, but gradually these will be replaced by voluntary post-factum payments, or second money.

The origins of second money deserve to be commented on separately. It has long been recognised on an intuitive level that culture needs its own regulator, in some ways analogous to money. Everybody involved in this realm has overtly or covertly suffered from the lack of a tool which would enable them to compare non-material values with each other and also with material values. Since ordinary money was obviously not up to the job, a need was felt for "cultural money". Although the need was generally recognised, it was also obvious that any attempt to create it ex nihilo was doomed to fail. It was unclear, however, what the alternative was. Collaborative practice led to a situation where there was no need to invent it. It would be enough just to upgrade the use of existing money by introducing a retrospective scheme of payment for experience goods as the norm. Post factum gratuity payment would reflect the sum of consumer satisfaction. These extra payments can be implemented both within the collaborative system or outside it, as already practised on a mass scale by people giving financial or other support to initiatives they care about. Until these actions are included in a collaborative system, second money will not be able to perform its measurement function. Within the collaborative filtering option post factum payment is only partly voluntary because group stimuli and sanctions operate. Such nominally voluntary payments we call "second money", and that is where the future of symbolic exchange lies.

3.4.1 Multifunctionality of Second Money

Being able to measure the symbolic will cause a restructuring of all the markets and spheres of life involved. Until then, the symbolic realm will remain on the periphery of the empire of money, and money will assist in plundering the territory, like a colony, giving very little in return. Second money gives culture a chance to regain its sovereignty. As we have noted, one of the imminent metamorphoses is associated with trust advertising. There are other business innovations which promise major change in many markets: unmediated distribution with payment directly to the producer, and user certification of quality. The practical effect of the retrospective use of money will make itself felt only when it achieves the magnitude of an institution. Point-scale ratings in a recommender network are a step in this direction and through them the economic sense of post factum transactions will become clear, namely raising the efficiency of individual consumption. When the rating function is integrated with the function of post factum recompense to the creative artist, the points system will either be replaced naturally or supplemented by second money, bringing with it fully fledged monetary measurement.

Information economics theory tells us that money arose from the need to optimise exchange, to simplify the path of goods in hand to the person who needs them. Before money, this transition involved a succession of barter exchanges. A person organised a combination of preliminary exchanges in order to obtain goods which his opposite number, who possessed a good he required, would accept as payment. Money came into use primarily because it shortened this procedure, reducing it from many moves to two moves. Money reduced exchange to the two standard operations of buying and selling. The main idea behind money is that it makes possible the separation of an exchange in time and space. In order to do so it needs to be a transitional good with the power of universal exchange. Subsequently, two other functions were added to these initial functions of money as a means of circulation and measurement (which had enabled trade and commerce to get on their feet). It became also a means of payment and saving, as a result of which it became an inalienable part of the vast majority of transactions. The dazzling career of money is an example its offspring, second money, should imitate.

Second money will flourish on the same basis as brought money into use, the uncoupling of exchange. Whereas conventional money optimises material exchange, second money enhances symbolic exchange. As payment for information about the subjective quality of information, and making it possible instantly to choose the best options for expending time, it raises the liquidity of time. As already mentioned, an important factor is that this new measure does not arise in a vacuum but emerges from the already existent institution of money. A further advantage is that second money performs other functions, of which we can mention at least three: (1) payment for services of consumer navigation; (2) recompensing creators of products; (3) measurement of symbolic values. There is also the function of saving, or at least fixation of symbolic capital, discussed below. Second money is thus multifunctional, which was the very quality underpinning the vitality of conventional money.

The more diverse the applications of second money, the more straightforward its progress will be and the greater its chances of gaining acceptance. Accordingly, let us take a look at some other practical examples of the use of second money.

3.4.2 Monetising User Activity in Third-Generation Networks

When second money enters collaborative practice, the question will arise of whether to restrict the size of post-factum payments. If they are not regulated, and there seems to be no reason why they should be, people will be able to donate however much they consider appropriate, irrespective of normative frameworks which are difficult to define to everybody's satisfaction. It will be found that, for a given level of satisfaction, well-to-do people are able to transfer more for a given product than those less well off. Accordingly, the effect of wealth will make itself felt. This will, on the one hand, complicate the game, but on the other it will offer some interesting possibilities. Despite people's anxieties, amounts of different value will not particularly inhibit the work of the collaborative mechanism, since proximity of tastes does not imply absolute coincidence of user profiles. It is enough for them to be similar, and the computer algorithms are capable of detecting just that. However, in measuring the symbolic capital of goods and services the effect of wealth does need to be taken into consideration because it is proportionate to the sum of gratuity payments. Otherwise, we will find that if we take two works, one of which has been liked by people who are not well-off while the other has been equally liked by prosperous people, the former will lose out solely because its admirers have less money at their disposal for expressing appreciation. Does this mean that it has produced less effect on their souls and is less valuable? Probably not. If the differentiation of preferences does not correlate with the level of income or the same works are liked by rich and poor in equal measure, this distortion will not arise. However, it is not worth trying to calculate everything while "standing on the riverbank". As soon as the system gets working, answers will be found to such questions. What we can say with all certainty at the present time is that monetary capital will be pumped over to symbolic capital and vice versa, and the result will be a better balance of each.

Post factum supplementary payments give solidity to a personal profile relative to a profile constructed solely on the basis of points. The actions of freeloaders underpaying for works they have liked could corrupt the system, but as a consequence the freeloader would incur costs in the form of poor quality recommendations and being ejected from the group. He faces the prospect of an inglorious demotion. Such is the basic defence of the collaborative system against parasites. Other defence mechanisms exist, based on the business motivation of users. As the experience of recommendation sites shows, a collaborative system can function effectively on points. At least, it can until it treads on the toes of affected industries by discrediting part of their output in the eyes of the public, which until then had been conscientiously paying up. At which point the industries will decide to smash the site. With the introduction into the system of money, recommender activity acquires its own business model whereby creators of information are rewarded in proportion to their contribution. A portion of post factum supplementary payments is directed to them, donated by users for the products they have recommended. We can and must see recommenders as conduits to a given good and, like any business facilitator, they have a right to an agent's commission. Apart from commission payments, payment may be made to them directly out of gratitude, putting them on equal terms with the creators of products and services. This is logical, taking account of the fact that a good pointer is sometimes no less valuable than the object it points to. And if it makes sense to pay for high-quality information, why not pay also for information about the quality of information?

Since behind every recommendation there are specific people (those taste neighbours of the user on whose judgements it is based), it is possible to distribute post factum money to individuals without any kind of arbitrariness, on a purely market basis. A particular recommender's share will depend in the first place on his contribution to the prediction (which we recall is dependent on the taste proximity of the recommender and recipient). In the second place, it will depend on the time when the rating is uploaded. Pioneering raters should be given encouragement. Additionally, the recompense can be increased in proportion to the size of the post factum payment a particular recommender made to reinforce his judgement (and that sum is unlimited). For example, if one of two recommenders has "staked" ten times more money on a work than a second, then, other things being equal, his shareholder's stake in the prediction should be that amount greater, as should his part of the income received for the prediction. Post factum money is thus not a slice of forfeited income but a kind of stake in a futures derivative which returns income if there proves to be a demand for the user's prediction. There is a kind of reciprocity: supplementary gratuity payments boomerang back to those who pay. This is a magical quality fundamental to the practice of sponsorship and donation which in no way detracts from their sincerity or attractiveness. At the present time it is difficult to calculate all the consequences of paying recommenders, but overall this scheme unambiguously strengthens the institution of collaborative filtering.

This business model has nothing in common with past attempts to create a cultural stock market to accept predictions of future box office takings from movies in the process of being made. That was reminiscent of a racing totalisator and did not yield good results, principally because the gamblers were not creating any useful information. In our case what we are looking at is not guesswork but the exchange of actual experience, and that radically alters the situation.

3.4.3 Symbolic Capital and Symbolic Values

In addition to symbolic values there is one further category which it is worth learning to measure, and that is the symbolic capital of various people. This is the ability of a person to produce symbolic value: works of art, maxims, texts, communications, anything which engenders quality time which can be measured in second money. Basing ourselves on the assumption that symbolic capital and second money correlate in the same way as ordinary capital and profit, we can put a value on symbolic capital. For this we can make use of existing practice: ordinary capital is assessed by its ability to generate profit, and symbolic capital should be quantified correspondingly in terms of revenue from second money.

Viewed in terms of the production of quality time, symbolic capital and symbolic values are kindred concepts. The difference is that the former is more a potential, while the latter is its realisation. A person possessing symbolic capital produces texts (in the broad sense of the word) and these, in proportion to their value, engender quality time. In actual fact the relationship here is more complex and less clear: works engender quality time and so does the creative artist himself, sometimes directly, without creating a work. His own behaviour is a kind of text. An evening in the company of a major personality is an example of how symbolic capital can translate directly into value. At the same time, a text can be a component of symbolic capital. It is not too much to say that not only a creative artist can possess symbolic capital, but so can the products of his creativity. In order to avoid confusion, however, we shall reserve the term "symbolic capital" for the person, and use the term "symbolic value" in respect of creations, whether these exist in verbal, written, or plastic form. Until capital is mobilised for the production of values, while it is awaiting its moment, it exists only in potential and it is impossible to form a judgement about it. In just the same way, symbolic values sometimes have to wait for their time to come and for them to be appreciated as they deserve.

But even when capital is vested in some kind of form and presented to the public, it is still impossible to measure it with the kind of accuracy we are accustomed to in operations involving conventional capital, because it is difficult to predict the return from it. Texts are an objective manifestation of symbolic capital. To continue the parallel with conventional economics, this is a product created in use.

Symbolic capital encompasses the whole spectrum of human attributes affecting the ability to create high-quality communications. These include experience, knowledge, taste, social competence, motivation, charisma, talent, and many other human qualities. Making use of these assets and basing himself on already existing texts, a person creates new texts which possess greater or lesser value, and which circulate in broad or narrow circles. It is not possible to dissect symbolic capital, to weigh its various constituents, but it can be rated overall on the basis of values created with its involvement.

All the symbolic values ever created add to the corpus of culture, increasing its total symbolic capital and preparing the way for the appearance of new values. Symbolic capital, like economic capital, is not self-sufficient: its generative, creative capacity is dependent on external factors, in particular such cultural institutions as (primarily) copyright, the material infrastructure, and the intellectual state of society. A potential movie maker of genius will have no career in a country without a cinema industry and (in all probability) probability theory would not have occurred to Pascal had he not had the game of dice to ponder.

It is of great practical importance that the series "symbolic capital–symbolic product–symbolic effect" leads to a category which can be measured: quality time. If we start from this end, we can quantify the two preceding links. From payment for quality time we can deduce a magnitude for the values which generated the quality time, and from these values we can deduce symbolic capital. In economics the technique for doing this is known as the earnings multiples approach and it is used for valuing businesses. Suppose a business is valued at ten times the annual profit it makes (this multiple depends on the riskiness of the business segment concerned), then the capitalisation of a firm which makes a profit of 1 million a year can be assessed at 10 million.

When speaking of symbolic value we are usually thinking of large, socially significant works, but the term should be understood more broadly: a great variety of manifestations of personality can engender quality time – oral performances or talks, public or private actions, – but irrespective of the kind of communication, a sign of value is a positive response from other people. Needless to say, the degree of influence exercised depends on the size and composition of the perceiving audience.

Symbolic capital is the engine of the New Economy. Just the fact of recognising that it is not only established creative artists who possess it but also ordinary people, is an important step. Ordinary people also emit information and, despite the difference in the power of the effect they produce, they can be included within a single system of symbolic coordinates and ranking. This reflects positively on the self-respect and motivation of members of communities. It is highly relevant to both professional and amateur creative artists, and indeed to people who are neither. In the past symbolic capital was considered the province of an elite but now we find that everybody possesses it. That does not mean that differences between people have been erased, but they are mitigated and from qualitative differences they become merely quantitative differences with many steps and gradations. This enables us to get away from a rigorous division into the first rate and lower levels, which in the past clipped the wings of many people.

With the transfer of activity to web networks, the barriers and distances between people decrease in just the same way as for a business when it enters the stock market. The difference between the founding owners of the company and its shareholders in the general population is evened out, and the transition from one status to the other becomes a matter of quantity. Something analogous brings about the appearance of web media, which are more influential than the traditional mass media.

Although the value of the individual is a widespread postulate in present-day society, it remains largely declarative or only occasionally evident, rather than being something that people really have any sense of. If symbolic capital is measured and presented objectively, this may facilitate a transition from good intentions to actual practice. Given the prospect of social and group recognition, people may develop a taste for a symbolic career. Symbolic stratification is a real need in society, and felt all the more acutely as new groups organise themselves. Objective measurement may provide a crucial impulse. The conditions for this already exist, with communications and the attitudes towards them documented in third-generation social networks. There is every reason for one of the important subsystems for measuring symbolic capital, personal reputation, to emerge in these networks.

3.4.4 Symbolic Capital and the Reputation System

Reputation is what other people think about the merits or demerits of a person, an institution, a business or a good. As regards people, reputation is part of their symbolic capital. It represents a projection of their symbolic capital into a particular sphere of activity and is significant within the framework of a particular community. Reputation performs the important function of predicting and guaranteeing quality. When accessing any information, people trust it to the extent that its source has given a good account of itself in the past. Reputation grows out of attitudes towards earlier activity. To put it simply, most people trust what has proved trustworthy in the past. They trust, knowing that the possessor of their trust will think very carefully before saying or doing anything which might harm his reputation. Brands operate on the same principle: investments in making themselves well-known serve as a pledge of the reliability of the business.

The object of our interest is reputations in formal communicative systems, primarily on the internet where communications are documented and can be categorised. Reputations formed in everyday life from miscellaneous information are not considered here because of the difficulty of detecting them. Obviously, reputational hierarchies depend heavily on which transactions between participants are taken into account, how far they reflect the real relationship, and how much is left out. Naturally, the more representative the registered transactions and the more precisely they are interpreted, the more reliable the reputation. The citation indices used on scholarly publications are a method for calculating reputation as simple as they are crude. They take account only of references to publications, but as no allowance is made for whose judgement this reflects, that of a professor or of a first-year student, or of how significant the context is in which the quotation figures, important information is lost. This has negative consequences for scholarship.

Internet search systems have made great advances in this area, since the order in which they deliver website addresses and pages in response to user enquiries is linked to the reputation of the sources, which is something they first establish. The Google PageRank algorithm computes the significance of a particular internet page using the logic that if a page contains a link to another, it is giving that page its vote. The more votes a page collects, the more important it is assumed to be. Account is taken of the weight of the page which is voting. Search systems have also solved the problem of mutual backscratching, against which academic citation indices have no defence. These principles have acquitted themselves well in practice and should be used when calculating personal reputation in groups.

In social networks reputation has a particular applied significance since it indicates the "quality" of the person you are communicating with. The demand for such grading must be extremely high, and one can only express amazement that the most visited international and Russian social network sites make virtually no use of this tool. There may be a conscious reluctance to reveal who is who, a fear of scaring off a proportion of users by indicating their place in the insider hierarchy.

For obvious reasons, reputations are particularly important in recommender systems, and these have far more data on the basis of which to establish them. If all that is registered in conventional social networks is whether a user has said "thank you" and whether a posting has been awarded a plus or minus, on recommendation sites a whole range of transactions can be taken into account: a user expressed thanks, followed advice, gave a reference, positively or negatively rated a comment, text, or photograph, requested a recommendation, forwarded a posting, etc. A comprehensive system for calculating non-professional reputations is to be found on the Russian Imhonet website, where each of these standard actions carries a particular weighting, depending on how much it contributes to reputation. More than a dozen actions are identified and, just as in the search systems, mutual backscratching is identified and eliminated. Reputation calculated in this way also grades interest in the user and his reliability, so-called goodwill. This serves as a further line of defence for the social network from fakes, fictitious infiltrated users, whose task is to manipulate data in the interests of sundry groups.

In the generally accepted navigation systems which provide ratings, charts and the like, data about the source of information is lacking, and this seriously detracts from the information itself. One cannot tell whose opinion the ratings reflect, and in charts constructed on sales data it is not even clear whether the public finally gave a product a positive or negative assessment. In recommender systems everything is transparent: you can see who is awarding reputation, and how it is arrived at.

A person's reputation can be calculated not only in general but also in respect of particular areas of expertise in literature, cinema, wines, photography or whatever, but also in respect of groups within whose framework it matters. This is of fundamental importance, since reputation in general is one thing, while reputation in a particular area is quite another. One can compute the overall reputation of a group in the eyes of wider society (or of some segment of it). One can calculate reputation on the basis of particular areas of competence, since it is often the case that a person is strong in one respect, as a critic or populariser, but does not enjoy more general respect.

A multi-factor calculation of reputation is a step forward from anything that has been done in this area so far. Second money will allow us to further raise the quality of the computations. It will enable a network's participants to express their attitude to each other's actions or comments quantitatively. PageRank, although it takes account of the density of transactions, does not know how much reputation is communicated in each. This is inevitable, since the search engine is dealing with inanimate objects, and websites cannot be asked directly how well one thinks of another. Accordingly, the order in which search engines deliver information sources in response to user enquiries does not reflect reputation in its precise meaning. A collaborative system, on the other hand, operates with unambiguously treated signals from people, which enables it to replicate precisely the logic by which off-line reputations are built. If to this we add the difficulty of mechanically interpreting the aims of enquiries, we can see how search results might be improved. For this, search and recommender technologies should be brought together to place a collaborative superstructure over the search system. That is, first a search should be conducted using the customary methods, and then the sources found should be filtered with the aid of a collaborative algorithm, promoting to a place among the first entries for a particular user what has previously satisfied enquiries from his reference group. This could create a next generation search engine capable not only of selecting information sources, but also of delivering them in accordance with the priorities of each individual.

3.5 The Mechanism of Social Revolutions

3.5.1 Three Mechanisms for Social Innovation

We have discussed consumer testing, voluntary post-factum payment, new business models in the digital industries, and other innovations which in the near future will be widely implemented. These are topics which impinge directly on business interests and are accordingly being actively discussed in professional circles and the media. The latter are, of course, themselves at the epicentre of events and seriously concerned that the content they create migrates to the internet, there to be consumed free of charge. The digital sphere which created the problems is likely to be the first to find a solution to them.

The question is, how and when will this occur? The practices and norms of behaviour described above are subject to a network effect: the more people profess them, the greater their value for each individual and therefore the more assured is their growth. While there are still not enough people involved, the web (like a club) is not all that exciting a place to be. A telephone would be no use if you were the only person who had one, which meant there was nobody to call. The system of collaborative filtering does not generate high-quality recommendations if it only has a few users. This is the so-called "cold start" problem. One has to surmount a certain quantitative barrier before stable, self-willed growth will occur. The new group will accumulate the critical mass of supporters required for lift-off only when a sufficient number of people believe in its value, and this comes through its being used. There is a chicken and egg situation here. The difficulty of institution building (as of any innovation) is precisely the synchronicity of these processes. From time to time, however, the new does manage to break through. Of particular interest are changes which are not imposed from above but grow from the grassroots, free activity of people, and this is a characteristic of the New Economy. Such novelties are closely linked to the mood of the masses, which in turn is associated with the dissemination of information within a society. The mechanisms of dissemination have been one of the least studied aspects of social life, hence the groundbreaking nature of the research discussed above. At the same time we have stressed that the most convenient bridgehead for such experiments is social networks on the internet. We need only to decide what to focus on, which is what we will do now.

There are many reasons why it is desirable to have an understanding of the mechanism of social start-ups, and to be aware of the conditions under which the institutions of the New Economy (collaborative filtering and micro-patronage) can take off is important for the present investigation also. This is what we need to concentrate our efforts on.

Much remains obscure about how institutions, standards and customs emerge, even when this occurs right under our noses, to say nothing of the distant past. Familiarising ourselves with existing descriptions of this process, we often have the impression that something fundamentally important, something decisive for the outcome, is being missed. Sometimes social consciousness registers the fact of the birth of institutions only after a long delay. Even when they are up and running, it is by no means the case that they are immediately understood. For example, the importance of even such an exceptional invention as the department store was not fully understood or appreciated at the time. There was, after all, more to the idea than merely offering a variety of goods in a compact area, which had already been done in ancient markets. The department store (one of the first opened in Milan in the second half of the eighteenth century) caused an information revolution by reducing transaction costs of haggling for the best price. Before this, the shopkeeper himself haggled with the customer, which meant he was constantly busy. In a department store prices are fixed and openly displayed, so there is no need to haggle. This makes it possible to put a less qualified person behind the counter while the entrepreneur gets on with expanding his business. A similar benefit, from the viewpoint of the customer, was that previously sorting matters out with the shopkeeper was the duty of the lady of the house, whereas now the servants could be dispatched to shop in the department store.

Or another example, image advertising. For a long time economists were perplexed by whether this was a form of coercion of customers. It was decided that it was a fundamental institution with roots in the most ancient practices of sacrifice. By paying for this, the advertiser was giving a pledge which signalled the quality of his goods. (A substantial contribution to the theory of this kind of signal was made by Michael Spence, one of the pioneers of information economics theory.)

The promotion of institutional innovations, and of particular techniques to enable them to enjoy a viral distribution, comes almost entirely under the heading of search and serendipity rather than of routine technology. There was a particularly dense fog surrounding the early stages of the process, and this drew our attention to the theory of superstars, snowball theory, and cheap talk theory, which were elaborated in connection with such situations. They were all formulated at different times, but for us what matters is to link them together and apply them to a wide range of phenomena. Although by and large only the theory of superstars can be considered a real theory (and that only at a pinch), while the other two concepts are one step down, the significance of this trio for understanding social evolution can hardly be overstated. I am certain they deserve to be far more widely known and receive a great deal more attention than they do at present.

The central question addressed by the theory of superstars is, why, out of numerous representatives of the creative professions, are particular individuals found at the top who are being paid astronomical sums? This is much the same question as we are interested in: why do certain innovations take off, while others do not? One of the explanations, propounded at various times by Adam Smith, Alfred Marshall, and Sherwin Rosen, comes down to the fact that several run-of-the-mill singers cannot replace a single Chaliapine. Because of immense demand, an outstanding talent becomes a superstar. This thesis is not entirely convincing. If at a given moment there is a shortage of Chaliapines, the stars do not disappear. Sheer force of talent, at first sight the obvious and self-evident explanation, will not do. It might close off the argument if somebody was head and shoulders above the rest and a star of the first magnitude, but such instances are rare. Far more typical is a situation where a pool of competitors is in no wise inferior to the leaders and would seem perfectly well able to attain those heights, only it doesn't happen. A huge disparity in salaries may (and does) occur even when there is no particularly marked difference in talent. Moshe Adler associated the limited number of stars with the limited space on the Mount Olympus of social attention. Consumers do not need an infinite proliferation of celebrities, because then it would be difficult to find someone else to discuss them with. If everybody chose their own star, conversation would dry up.

This explanation is wholly in the spirit of the group economy: empathising with popular performers, being up-to-date on hot topics, works, events, enables people to minimise the costs of making and maintaining contacts. The motive behind such synchronisation of preferences is rational use of such resources as attention, memory and time.

People have a great urge to socialise, and what provides the excuse is not all that important. A superstar is created, not so much because of the performer's inherent qualities, as by the need to satisfy a demand, that is, an extraneous factor from the sphere of information economics. Similar considerations apply to omens and superstitions, whose specific semantic content is fairly arbitrary but whose purpose is to reduce the number of options of behaviour, and thereby the costs of choosing. This probably all sounds a bit odd, but everything falls into place if we treat human attention as a resource for which the competition is no less fierce than for customers with disposable income. The fact that the explanations proposed by the theory of superstars do not seem obvious only shows how novel the logic of the New Economics still is.

If superstars are recruited from a pool of people of approximately equal talent, how come one of them rises to the first magnitude? The answer is to be found in the metaphor of the snowball, which explains the ultimate breakthrough into popularity as being due to an advantage at the start. The handful of snow which starts rolling first gets more snow stuck to it faster and more easily, and leaves less behind for its laggard competitors. As applied to top internet sites, this means a critical mass of users has been acquired who have mastered the useful functions, become familiar with the layout, provided themselves with contacts ("friends"), and communicated something about themselves. In a word, they have built a home in cyberspace. For a competing resource to lure these people away needs a Herculean effort, which can be theoretically quantified as the time and money the user will need to spend in order to adapt to a new site. Let us suppose that it is going to take 2 h to become familiar with the new place and sort everything out. If we treat this as low-paid work and assess it at a rate of $5 an hour, then to attract a single user will cost a minimum of $10. In practice the sum will be higher, because something needs to be added by way of compensation for emotional attachment to the earlier habitat which the user is being asked to sacrifice. The cost of attracting that first, most difficult, million users adds up to a very appreciable sum. In addition, those creating the network do not know exactly when or how they will be able to convert the heads they have hunted into revenue.

It is still unclear, however, why one particular handful of snow should be the first to start rolling. The theory of superstars has no answer, although from a practical point of view this is a crucial issue. In order to find the answer, let us turn to the concept of "cheap talk" from game theory, where the term is applied to communication at the start of a match which determines its course. A textbook example is bluff in a game of poker. Economists have already used the term "cheap talk" to explain the success of advertising campaigns in which magical qualities are ascribed to goods and a unique aura to brands (Birger Wernerfelt). For example, a certain company claims that people who buy its products will find the solution to some kind of insoluble problem in their life. For certain users, gullible or who merely enjoy trying out anything new (and 2 or 3% of society consists of such people), this is enough to make them choose the product, despite the fact that the producer's assurances may be entirely groundless. Hence the epithet "cheap", because unproven. If a sufficient number of such people is acquired, the snowball is on its way. Thereafter it grows without outside help in accordance with the scenario described above. A claim, thrown out into society virtually at random, gains weight and may become a self-fulfilling prophecy. This is how certain goods focus demand on themselves. On the whole, it is to the advantage of customers because the price will go down. The same applies to ideas and rules of behaviour. If everywhere one constantly hears that gentlemen prefer blondes, they really will.

If a horoscope prescribes that a capricorn is steadfast and an aquarius contrary, that is often how they will be perceived. A necessary condition for bringing people with similar preferences together is to identify a cause and a rallying point for the first adherents. It is relatively easier for others to join the pioneers, and the numbers swell in accordance with snowball logic. People prefer the most successfully launched goods and brands, despite the fact that others available at the time may be no worse. Thus does "cheap talk" act as an impeller to get things going, and thereafter the course of events can be directed along a desired scenario. The same result is achieved by extravagant advertising, a path chosen by producers confident of the quality of their goods, and also by those who find it most convenient to make a pledge through image advertisement to persuade people of the quality of their goods. Out of context and without an understanding of the role ascribed to it, "cheap talk" looks arbitrary and fairly senseless, but in fact it does make sense, and considerable sense at that. It focuses people's attention on a relatively small number of alternatives and minimises the delays and costs of choosing.

3.5.2 The Art of "Talk" in Contemporary Art

The range of phenomena where the logic of cheap talk operates is extensive and includes, for example, political and stock market processes, scientific doctrines, a variety of subcultures and much else. These, if not viewed from the perspective of the trio of theories we are considering, can seem to be merely the play of chance or a scenario rigorously programmed by circumstances. Certain sectors, for example, sport, where in most cases quality is objectively registered, are relatively immune to the influence of injections of information. Even in sport, however, winners are sometimes "appointed", and even in engineering technology, which would appear to be wholly resistant to manipulation, "cheap talk" plays no small part. It finds scope, for example, where there needs to be a decision on the financing of a particular technological policy and where the merits of the alternatives are not, at that moment, entirely obvious.

As regards contemporary art, "cheap talk" has acquired such power that it often stands in for the works themselves. Artists organise surprising actions, for example, wrapping buildings or bridges in cellophane, or exhibiting doggie doo and seek thereby to shift the boundaries of perception of the public. Pictures, installations and performances may be full of profound meaning (like, no doubt, the above-mentioned works which all caused a great stir at the time), or they may have a less impressive content or even have no meaning at all, amounting to the purest placebo.

Their mission is to assemble a group of people, and it doesn't much matter if the king is found to be wearing no clothes. Taken outside the logic of group or club communications, the happening may have no significance whatsoever.

The apotheosis of this tendency has been the flash mob event, during which people get by admirably without an artist. All they need is a coordinating signaller. Indeed, if at one time artists rejected form, then content, why are they now needed at all? Matters have developed to a point where their services are rejected. Why should the public not ask, "What's so special about him? We've got polythene too".

In the spectrum of emotions evoked by contemporary art, awe is far from enjoying first place. This has facilitated the appearance of a new trend in culture. While the artist was surrounded by an aura of unattainability, seen as God's elect, expected to produce a shock effect on viewers, few ventured to try their strength as creators and appear in public. As soon as this restriction was lifted, a great flood of amateur creativity washed over culture. In part this brought about the burgeoning of the blogosphere, where users do their darnedest to create their own flash mobs and to glory in their moment of fame. This also explains the exaggerated popularity of broadcasts in which dilettantes squawking like chickens sing some mediocre ditty and the audience joins in. A revival of amateur artistic activity is occurring on an amazing scale, and although at first the downside of the process is more in evidence, in future this will benefit culture, including its more exalted realms. Just as football in the courtyard feeds into the national team, so karaoke produces at least excellent listeners. Taking part is far more positive than passive viewing, although at the present stage there are some grounds for concern since the pyramid of taste is sinking towards its base and showing no signs of rebounding any time soon.

While the masses, having gained a different level of access to culture, are trying their strength in creativity and deliriously pursuing recognition at group level, those for whom artistic creativity is their bread and butter are selling out. They are increasing their output and producing weaker and weaker products. A host of competitors of a new kind is taking a slice of the attention market away from them and the quality gap between what they and their rivals produce is narrowing. With the appearance of Web 3.0 tools, users are taking over the function of experts and discovering talent themselves, putting publishers under pressure. Similar threats hang over writers, at least those of average or little talent. They are being successfully replaced by bloggers. If by and large the democratisation of culture can only be welcomed, one hopes that artists will not surrender to cheap talk to the extent that they are reduced to the status of a beacon for someone else.

3.5.3 "Cheap Talk" as a Signal to Diverge?

In the theory of superstars the sequence of cause and effect is reversed: the actual qualities of an object mean little by comparison with the dynamics of its popularity. This provocative thesis not only throws light on the origins of superstars but also enables us to look differently at a whole swathe of social phenomena where we are puzzled that the situation has resolved itself in one way rather than another. Where there is a sheaf of possible scenarios, there is always a cheap talk competition to decide the winner. This process is not as random as many people believe.

The spring which drives the mechanism is that human need for high-quality, congenial contacts which is satisfied by joining a suitable community. Superstars, brands, religious trends, political parties, fan clubs (and also such issues as whether to eat your boiled egg from the big end or the little end, or how to perform religious rituals): it is all a matter of finding ways to split up into groups, thus optimising one's social habitat. No small contribution to this is made by art, which thereby demonstrates its social credentials. Artists are emitters of artistic statements and the public serve as a filter which allows works through or blocks them depending on how far they meet their need for social consolidation or fragmentation. On the whole it does not really seem to matter so much what the issue is, so long as it is presented starkly. This will prove the occasion for people who are in some respect outsiders to differentiate themselves from others, to diverge, and for those with some degree of kinship to coalesce. In retrospect researchers imbue clashes which played a notable role in history with portentous meaning, but the truest and deepest meaning is simply that a question is openly raised which provokes people into thinking, deciding their position, and adhering to one side or the other.

Facing people with a dilemma is an ancient and infallible method of dividing society into camps based on the documented attitude of people to a doctrine, a topic, facts, or a ritual. This same universal technique is at the basis of today's mutual filtering, which people use on each other and in which all manner of means of attracting one's own sort of person are brought to bear: dress, manners, actions, provenance, links with mates from school and college, and general acquaintances. In the computerised version, selection is conducted also along lines of tastes, preferences and interests. The organic way in which collaborative filtering is spreading on the internet derives from the fact that precisely these procedures (only more spontaneously and less consciously) have always been used. Present-day technologies have merely automated and perfected them.

3.5.4 Social Imprinting

If everything relating to the formation of superstars was really so much a matter of technique and the knack was merely to get known first, why would not everybody try their luck? Alas, the trick is not so much getting off to a quick start as managing to pluck the right heartstrings, since otherwise the snow (the resource of attention) will not stick. The trio of laws described above gives no guidance as to what happens at the very earliest, embryonic, prenatal stage of preference formation, and yet this is precisely what will decide which offering of cheap talk will be taken up. Without this link the whole chain of deductions is like a rope ladder which does not quite reach to the ground. This link, I suggest, is related to imprinting, which was popularised by Konrad Lorenz.

The essence of this phenomenon is conveyed by a photograph which has found its way into the textbooks: it shows Lorenz walking along, followed by a group of goslings. It transpires that, shortly after hatching, goslings seek the image of their mother. They identify her solely because she is the first thing that moves in their field of vision, and follow her. It is important who or what that first thing is. In the experiment it was Lorenz, and the goslings were drawn after him as if after their biological mother. His place could equally well have been taken by a moving balloon. They would have accepted that and, having made their choice, would have completely ignored their real mother if they met her.

3.5.4.1 Imprinting in Man

Imprinting has been most fully studied in animals. It has been established that before they appear in the world their first steps are programmed in the form of a collection of reactions to the conditions they are going to meet. These investigations, together with much valuable information about instincts and the organisation of the brain, have enabled us to unlock the secret of how canaries sing, and to explain how a salmon travels all the way back to its long abandoned birthplace to lay its eggs. The topographical sense of bees and wasps is also a result of imprinting. As regards human beings, they have been studied less since one has to be considerably more circumspect in handling them. A researcher is hardly going to shove some inanimate object in front of an infant in a bid to replace its mother. Although it would seem that for a whole variety of institutions which fish for human beings (politicians, traders, clergymen) there could be nothing more tempting than learning how to programme personality and mould character.

For all the sparsity of the data about imprinting in man, the mechanism is so important for the New Economy that it is worth trying to generalise everything which in one way or another relates to it.

We know that people are more vulnerable to imprinting in certain states of mind, which leads to an ineradicable acceptance of something. During these particular periods in their life, certain images, positive or negative, can become fixated. These then assume an unchallengeable significance for the person and this persists for many years, predetermining principles, inclinations, methods of perception and so on. Periods of particular impressionability are found mainly in infancy, and to a lesser extent in early adulthood. Something similar to imprinting does, however, also occur later, although in a less pronounced form. In infants subsequent social conditioning has yet to blur the picture, so they have been studied more and with greater success. In adults imprinting tends to be confusingly overlaid by other effects (which does not mean that it is not there). Something which supports the view that late imprinting exists is the fact that certain mental techniques make reimprinting possible (Timothy Leary), that is, reprogramming the alignment of an individual's personality. The practice of conditioning a person away from alcoholism is probably a phenomenon of this category. Imprinting in man is not a lifelong trap, but immense efforts are needed to escape from it. Occasionally this does happen spontaneously over time. It has been established in recent years that it is possible to deliberately edit memory with the assistance drugs. Unlike the inducing and development of conditioned reflexes, as studied in Pavlov's dogs, with imprinting the fixation is stamped on the personality on a single occasion, without repeated stimulation. The necessary condition for imprinting is an emotion which sears the depths of the soul, which is probably applicable to any persistent effect in the mind. The durability of an impression is always related to the strength of emotions, and these in turn depend on the mind's willingness to respond to the stimulus, and on its magnitude.

3.5.4.2 Narrative Knowledge About Imprinting

Psychology has neglected the topic of imprinting in man. Perhaps in the past there was a lack of suitable tools for such complex research, so that it was impossible to produce experiments which could be replicated. Today the issue just seems to be overlooked. The present-day economy is an interweaving of motivations and desires and, engaging with it, we simply cannot ignore what lies at the root of the forces which motivate a human being. Observations suggest that imprinting is fundamental to much of human behaviour, if less incontrovertibly than in our fellow animals.

The fact that psychology is ill-informed about imprinting does not mean that we do not meet its manifestations in everyday life. How many stories have we heard about how a child has developed an obsession. Some uncle eight times removed has appeared briefly in the family wearing his captain's cap and before you know it a boy is halfway to naval college. Something of the kind is behind the history of Peter the Great's toy flotilla, said to be behind his later love of the navy. Perhaps a boy has seen how girls his own age dress their dolls and much later discovers a predilection for that particular kind of appearance. The role of imprinting in matters of the heart is not entirely clear, but is certainly significant. At the very least it can be traced in the perception of types of beauty, which are laid down by toy factories and polished by advertisements and glossy magazines. And of course there is that fatal sensitivity, made the more powerful by long abstinence, which creates a fertile soil for love at first sight. Imprinting influences also the particulars of sexual behaviour. It seems that a majority of transvestites were dressed in clothing of the opposite sex in childhood. Another example, from the Middle Ages, tells how the sight of a naked body beaten with rods was a source of erotic stimulus for many. In the modern age, with the abolition of such public punishments, sexual perversion of this kind has become rarer. Relations between parents and children, etched in the subcortex, cause children when they grow up and themselves become parents, to replicate past experiences, negative as well as positive. Having suffered in the past, people are unable to free themselves from the programming.

Imprinting manifests itself in phobias and fears, in the mastering of languages and in many other ways. Various viral effects are evidently associated with it (including those on the internet), when some craze becomes instantly popular. Successful advertisement too cannot do without it. Delving back in memory, a person may sometimes resurrect some pivotal moment when a decision was suddenly ready to be adopted, or a new way of perceiving, or an attitude to the world (aesthetic, pragmatic, moral, religious, scientific), which became dominant. At some point in the distant past a switch became fixed at a certain position and the child grew up to be an activist or a conformist, preferred numbers or letters, inclined to a particular way of filtering information, or formulated questions to the world which would guide him for the rest of his life.

How educators would like to catch this moment and direct the child's powers in his best interests as seen by his parents! If only they could etch into his subconscious a "correct" attitude so that thereafter everything would go swimmingly and the person would absorb only what was wholesome. No such precedents are known. Influencing consciousness is the province only of specialists in the behavioural rehabilitation of alcoholics, and brand managers. When something is brought close to an infant's eyes or he has his attention focused on some detail, he is being given the keys for further, subsequent perception. Science does not, however, tell us how to manage imprinting. Nobody presumes to predict what will take with a particular person, or when.

3.5.4.3 Imprinting and Attention Economics

Much remains obscure about a person's imprinting, but one thing is not in doubt: it is linked to the mechanisms of decision making and hence plays a role in the economy of desires. It is of fundamental importance that, even before a person finds himself faced with a choice, he is largely preprogrammed, not only by ordinary, rational considerations but also by certain crucial episodes in his past or, more precisely, the imprints they have left in his mind. An economic logic can be found in imprinting itself. In essence it operates like an information filter, letting one thing through but blocking another. The whole system of personal attitudes may be regarded as a complex hierarchical filter. Along with early, basic imprints it includes later images, acquired reflexes, fixed fantasies, motivations – all of which determine attachments, habits, perception, character traits, and indeed the whole way of life. Each new imprint attracts or rejects, conditioning selectivity in the reception of information. There is thus a direct link between imprinting and attention economics. The mechanism simultaneously delimits permissible decisions and serves as a regulator of the intake of information. Without it the human brain would grind to a halt, unable to cope with the torrent of signals.

If we approach this field with strict criteria, only a fairly narrow circle of phenomena will be found to relate to imprinting as such, but a whole series of kindred mechanisms operate similarly, leaving impressions in the human mind. These traces may differ in depth and clarity and may result from repeated, deliberate conditioning rather than occurring as instantly and spontaneously as imprinting. There may be substantial differences between them and in how they affect consumer behaviour, but for the time being the mechanisms of impression have been insufficiently researched and we cannot fill in the detail. The main point is that, quite independently of marketing techniques for leaving impressions, the human mind is peppered with them. The moment decisions have to be taken, past impressions operate like railway points, directing actions along one track or another. The mechanisms of acceptance or non-acceptance also vary, depending on an unconscious willingness to allow something into oneself (imprinting) or a conscious opposition to, for example, advertising. We can draw an analogy with the procedure of weighing something, picturing the imprint as a heavy weight placed on the scales and all the other motivations in the form of makeweights added to one side or the other and overall adding up to a considerable weight in their own right.

As the personality develops, the system of filters which help the mind to process reality becomes more complex. New impressions are either overlaid on existing ones or are rejected by them. Before they are allowed to settle into the existent motivational framework, certain conditions have to be met and they have to cohere with previously acquired imprints. Dependent on that, certain impressions (motivations, desires, habits) find the road ahead open, while others find it closed. Imprints thus work directly on their own account, but also indirectly by programming subsequent inclinations. These fundamental and derivative impressions are consolidated in the mind as habits and a way of life and are interlinked by a thousand different threads. You cannot just tear one out of the fabric. A person who is overweight will find it difficult to decide simply to give up eating an evening meal. If an innovation conflicts with the system of impressions already established, the latter will try to nullify it.

3.5.4.4 From Imprinting a Person to Imprinting a Society

Imprinting can be found also in a society. It influences the direction taken when there is a fork in the road of history. When they try to interpret such moments, people often talk about providence or chance, but imprinting suggests a different explanation. At the social level this mechanism manifests itself in the totality of imprints most frequently encountered in people, in basic values and ethnic stereotypes which regulate many different spheres: the attitude to love, discipline, faith, puritanism or hedonism, usury, a leadership-or-community orientation. This amalgam is given the somewhat outmoded title of national character. Common morality arises from the synchronised imprints received from a shared environment with stimuli which are similar for everybody. Cliches are drawn from language, folklore, texts and everyday life, from "culture" in its broadest sense. Life sets traps for the mind, but also helps it to become receptive (imprint vulnerability), creating a tension if something is lacked and as a result evoking a dramatic emotional reaction when a desired stimulus occurs. In different geographical regions the mind of a child is "stamped" in different ways. The national way of life has its unique primary socialisation of children. Local norms of swaddling, hygiene, safety, obedience and independence, cuisine informed by maternal warmth, the culture of emotional upbringing within the family, these are the rocks to which personality is anchored.

Since the norms of everyday life are the same for everyone and permeate all layers of society, this cumulation of deeply buried stereotypes awaiting their hour is also largely homogeneous.

Imprints are synchronised within one generation but are transformed by the next. Conditions change, and by no means all the images which so captivated parents can be handed on in the relay race. Descendants are not receptive to all of them. The imprinted images of generations differ all the more strongly if the realities of childhood years have been greatly different. The experience which parents have accumulated may prove invalid under new conditions. The changes which have taken place in the digital age have engendered a so-called prefigurative culture, a situation where less that is useful can be passed from parents to children than would have been the case if change had been less abrupt.

Intergenerational fractures have occurred in the past, as an extensive literature testifies, but today's is unusually complete because of unprecedented changes related to a sharp rise in the productivity of labour and a change in the way leisure time is used. There is now more free time than working time. The emphasis has moved from work to consumption, from saving to spending, with a corresponding transformation of morals. This, indeed, is what has brought about the New Economy, and a marked re coding of personality.

3.5.4.5 Imprinting and "Cheap Talk"

We have dwelt in detail on imprinting in order to explain why in certain instances "cheap talk" takes off, while in others it remains mere hot air. A certain percentage of people in society are receptive to the new. If cheap talk falls on fertile imprinting ground, these people will easily overcome the inertia of an easy life and comprise an initiative group capable of growth. Since much "talk" is going on at any given moment, some of it will hit the target, like a bullet from a random burst of machine-gun fire. People need to be "hit" in this way because, for a group economy to function, a certain rate of renewal of communities is essential. New codes are devised so that, when a club becomes too full, its leaders can use them to partition themselves off again. From numerous alternatives, the one adopted is the one which meets an unconscious demand rooted in new imprints. A process is initiated in the social cauldron with its law of large numbers which it is difficult to replicate under laboratory conditions. Such an interpretation of innovation is at variance with the popular viewpoint, which sees novelties as a single, calculated shot from a sniper. In reality, the birth of innovations is a two-stage process of emission and filtration. The first phase is the production of trial offerings, while the second is collective selection. Creativity is itself a two-stage process. Ideas enter a person's head and he mentally filters them until he arrives at an insight. To start a "talk" and present it to society for judgement is the first part of the task, and that is the responsibility of the inventor, the creative individual. No less important, however, is the second part where one particular "talk" is taken up out of the many. This is the stage at which social imprints come into play.

A community develops its own system of filters, and until a happy combination of these is found a high-quality idea usually has to wait. Sometimes the moment is irrevocably lost. Just as a person with his bounded rationality makes do with an option which is satisfactory rather than ideal, so the community sometimes cannot wait for an ideal solution. An institutional trap appears: if some norm has become firmly established in practice, it is difficult for an innovation to displace it. If one scenario has been realised, it is difficult to move to another one, even if the latter is objectively better (Douglass North). In just the same way, people find it difficult to change their habits because they become encrusted with a host of other habits, practices, and obligations. The textbook example is the QWERTY keyboard which goes back to the days when mechanical typewriters were being distributed. More ergonomic keyboards have been proposed (for example, the COLEMAK layout), but we continue to use the old layout because everybody has got used to it. Today's users prefer not to relearn. Manufacturers have to take account of this and block innovation, afraid of weak demand.

It would be interesting to estimate the qualitative characteristics of imprinting and, in particular, to understand what is needed to get people to start the juggernaut of innovation moving. The sociology of fashion (and fashion is intimately linked to imprinting) enables us to estimate the number of groups which are potential carriers of a "virus". Fashion innovators (those particularly susceptible to innovation) are approximately 2–3% of the market. After them come early adopters, 10–15%, then the fashion followers – up to 35%, and finally the laggards – 35%. The latter two groups, which comprise a total of 70% of the market, are those who will take up a trend in the course of a year to 18 months. The remaining 13%, conservatives, do not join in the game. It is not impossible that 2–3% (or thereabouts) is a universal number which determines the size of a target group receptive to "cheap talk", not only in fashion but also in other areas. Thereafter the innovation is capable of spreading under its own steam.

If we suppose that the 2–3% mentioned are sufficient to launch a variety of processes, the question arises of why precisely this number of adepts is capable of acting as a catalyst for subsequent steady growth. We may suppose that if an innovation has caught the imagination of 2 or 3 people out of every 100, then this will become known in one way or another to their close circle. Because this averages several dozen individuals for each of them, through direct interpersonal contacts news of the innovation will reach the whole 100, and everybody who so wishes will be able to sign up. Needless to say, to create the critical mass it is essential to have that many people so that, through word of mouth, they are able to inform the rest of society. If what we have said is true, then a decisive role in the fate of "cheap talk" is played by a horizontal information cascade, that is direct communication between people. The vertical flow of information also exercises an influence. If powerful information channels like television are mobilised, then in order to launch a horizontal cascade fewer than 2% may be needed, and if it is not, more than 3% may be required.

3.5.4.6 Imprinting and Advertising

As noted above, economists explain branding in terms of "cheap talk". Brand managers rely on imprinting, sometimes deliberately but more often intuitively. The credo of designer logos is to coincide with people's latent expectations and transform the advertised good into a fetish. Spiderman, Bionicles from Lego, accessories for Barbie and other symbols of their time are directly inserted into people's subconscious. To the same category belongs the marketing of food additives which are parasitic on the health cult, the preaching of pseudo-religious theories, and other more constructive phenomena. The stage is taken not by random goods and services, but by those which appeal to particular mindsets. Moreover, it is a matter not of the rational expectations of a particular quality, with which conventional marketing operates, but of slumbering, deep images. The interconnections are often far from obvious. For example, it is claimed by branding specialists that for North Americans personal independence is associated, amongst other things, with toilet paper. Accordingly, advertising for this associates it with other attributes of independence. Peanut butter is associated with maternal warmth; Swiss watches, Belgian chocolate, Russian kvass, Italian spaghetti, French cheese and Chanel's little black dress are iconic goods different for each culture but deeply embedded in the system of associations.

Imprint favourites are associatively linked with a number of other goods and draw them in their wake, lighting them up with their aura. When market researchers question people as to what they would like their next car to look like, the answers by no means cover everything that will really influence them at the moment of choice. They talk out loud about the size of the luggage compartment and the position of the air intake, but actually picture themselves in a brutal jeep, heedlessly careering across the prairie, or dream of a retro limousine, James Bond's car, or an armoured car with the hatch raised. Their choice is determined by a cocktail of fantasy and common sense and, other things being equal, the company which gets the fantasies right is the one which makes the sale.

So when "cheap talk" engages with imprinting, the ignition fires. If we count up the total costs needed to bring these things triumphantly together, we will see that ultimately cheap talk works out far from cheap. Sometimes immense efforts and many attempts are needed to hit the G-spot and bond the image with subconscious aspirations. The weaker the message and the less accurate its targeting, the more repetition is needed to lodge it in people's heads. Success comes not only to dazzling advertising campaigns but to many others. It just costs the less talented ones a whole lot more.

3.5.5 An Illustration From Science of Phase Transformations in the Community

The plan of social innovations proposed needs further work and needs to be made more precise. In particular, the snowball analogy, on closer inspection, proves more delightful than accurate. The automatic further growth of communities after a critical mass of supporters has been reached is seen as self-evident, but real snowballs as they roll downhill increase only to a certain size, after which they cease to grow. Why, then, do social snowballs keep growing to avalanche proportions? The analogy looks only at the raw competitive advantage of the first snowball which deprives the others of snow, but the actual growth process is not considered at all. What does the critical mass depend on? Is the number of people in the community important or are there other factors?

In order to answer these questions, let us resort to an illustration from natural science, from solid body physics. Such parallels are considered questionable, but nevertheless the restructuring of inanimate matter strikingly resembles the processes in society and helps us to make out what is going on. In some respects atoms do behave like living beings: they are not indifferent to their environment, they can change their neighbours, separate into groups with a different mutual disposition, and block off enclaves with barriers or borders. In a word, they can do the same things as people in a community. As a result of such restructuring, caused by a change in external conditions, a solid body alters its interior structure and attributes. One of the main mechanisms for such transformation is the engendering and growth of new embryos. That is, just as in society, within an inanimate system there arise hearths of growth with different attributes which gradually expand to restructure and reconfigure the initial matrix in their own image.

Physicists have given this process an explanation which may be of interest for the humanities. The first experimentally established element is the need for acquisition of a critical mass. Under particular conditions all the atoms of a substance are drawn to assume a new structure, but the only communities successful are those which have attained a certain size. Having done so, they begin to grow steadily. Those which have not reached the necessary mass are re-absorbed by the initial matrix. The growth of viable conglomerates continues until they encounter other conglomerates similar to themselves, engendered in a different hearth and developing in parallel. At that moment the process of transformation ends, since there is nowhere further to grow. All the atoms have been allocated to communities.

Why do new embryos arise? This is explained by a gaining of energy in the new configuration (which results in a distance between the atoms being established which is optimal for the new conditions). Putting it very simply, in this new distribution the atoms feel better than they did in the old one, and if we extrapolate this explanation to the community, a better group environment arises. Why are not all conglomerates inclined to grow, but only those sufficiently large, when it would seem to be equally advantageous for all to restructure? The obstacle proves to be the new surface (returning to our lexicon, the boundary of the group). At the boundary the new formation comes into contact with the initial mass and a tension arises there. Always and everywhere the abutting of the new and the old results in a problem zone. If we are talking of people they, as it were, find themselves falling between two stools. And if we are talking about particles of matter, then if in the border regions between them the distance is not optimal, extra energy has to be expended to keep them in that position. A small growth hearth may have insufficient resources to build its own boundary, which is essential for separation. The new, harmoniously constructed volume grows by a cubic function from its width, while its surface grows quadratically. But as at the start the quadratic outpaces the cubic, so the forces of surface tension hold back initial growth.

In other words, the larger the new formation, the fewer the number of its participants fated to live in the discomfort of the new frontier strip. Growth enters a steady phase when newbies immediately land in a favourable environment in such numbers that the heterogeneous neighbours have no impact. Until social density is sufficient, the ties of the past pull everything backwards.

We have deliberately anthropomorphised a natural process in order to emphasise similarities. Let us return to the social coordinates. The analogy of the energy advantage which moves particles is, in respect of new social group formations, improved quality of communications. People join a group because they see potential quality time for themselves within it. The group grows unobstructed from the moment new recruits arrive in a more or less comfortable environment. The main thing the group economy should learn from our analogy is the role of boundaries. Creating these requires an upfront investment. Historians say, "The rich get richer because they are rich". Correspondingly, the poor lock themselves inside a vicious circle of poverty. The analogy from physics allows us to develop this idea by pointing to the importance of barriers to growth.

The three mechanisms we have examined bring us to an understanding of how all sorts of doctrines, ideologies, beliefs, moral imperatives and the like crystallise out in the human mind and determine the behaviour of the masses and the course of history. "Cheap talk" gives rise to the "snowball", which in turn brings about the formation of "superstars", and the latter conquer hearts and minds which, for their part, are ready and waiting to be conquered. Social imprinting completes the chain and helps us to understand why one "talk" gets taken up while another does not.

3.6 Collaborative Filtering and the Prospects for Democracy

Collaborative filtering can also have political applications. In economics, the theory of social choice (propounded by James Buchanan and Gordon Tullok) analyses political institutions. Attempting to expound it here would serve no purpose, but it will be helpful to outline how collaborative technologies can be applied in this sphere.

The basic idea is that universal, unhampered and unmediated socialising of each with each and of each with all brings about major changes in the nature of the electoral environment: its coherence, informational conductivity, activity and reactivity will be increased many times over. If people are given the tools to unite in meaningful coalitions, the quality of the electoral process is likely to improve markedly. Rules and procedures for forming institutions of government are firmly tied to communication facilities and the sophistication of the electorate, and accordingly there will be a powerful impulse towards transforming these institutions. It is worth considering how the political (electoral) toolkit would be renewed, and possibly beginning to redesign it in advance, and even start trialling it.

If the technology of filtering had not been invented for resolving problems of consumer navigation in culture, it would need to be invented for developing democracy. We can detect the beginnings of collaborative filtering in the current procedures for elections: the electorate is grouped along territorial and party lines, although admittedly both are imperfect ways of aggregating interests. For example, living in the same region may imply a certain community of interests, but this is by no means total. Intellectuals in Kostroma and Vyatka may be far closer to each other than to their neighbours from other social strata. As regards the division into parties, it faces many people with a dilemma: whether to rally under the banner of the dissidents or abstain from voting. No small percentage of people chooses the latter of these two evils, finding no candidate they respect, or recognising that the one they do favour will not gain the necessary number of votes. In this way, their interests, and also the interests of others who voted for candidates who did not pass the prescribed threshold, are discriminated against. Possibly, if they lived in a region with a larger number of like-minded people, they would enjoy political representation. The party mechanism is also unsatisfactory because people do not know or understand the manifestoes, and the party leaders for their part do not know their supporters. Manifestoes are often a potpourri of "cheap talk", and moreover not in an academic but in the everyday sense of the expression.

For these and other reasons democracy works less well than it might. In the elections fewer political groups are participating than is essential for the process to work properly. Those which win prove unstable in their composition with the result that their work is less satisfactory. A political group is a means of aggregating the will of individuals and delegating it upwards for implementation. If the interests within the group are chaotic, they will cancel each other out and, instead of strength, what will be projected to the outside world is impotence (Mancur Olson). We can bring the ideal of democracy closer if we find a method of delivering political representation of many interest groups, each with its own clearly delineated interests. Then any citizen would have his own empowered representatives in the areas which matter to him, whether professional, educational, leisure, or other. Despite the utopian nature of the idea, it is gradually maturing in people's minds. The point is that a person, being a multifaceted individual, could divide his vote between the leaders of several electoral associations he favoured, each of which would specialise in particular interests: ethnic, business, cultural or sport, as long as it could assemble a sufficient number of supporters. In order to participate in these coalitions, a person would need to subscribe a quota of personal resources to each of them, thereby registering the degree of his interest, and naturally he would have to decide to which organisations he needed to, and could afford to, belong. The number of interest groups cannot proliferate infinitely. The process of fragmentation of society into parties is self-regulating. Moreover, the real (solvent) demand for democracy is revealed, and the extent to which society can afford it becomes visible. As a result, a political system would emerge which consisted of many blocs crisscrossing the electorate, each representing different aspects of their voters' interests. This scheme describes an extreme but imaginable development of democracy. The idyll is unlikely ever to be realised, not least because of the QWERTY effect, but it is nevertheless profoundly in harmony with the new group economy. Even if it will take a considerable time before actual moves in this direction occur, collaborative filtering (and we cannot do without it) will gradually begin to be enlisted in political practice. Since this is a technology for forming any group, it is in principle applicable also to political associations. One can foresee the following potential effects: (1) voters would group more meaningfully, since groups will be formed in full view of them; (2) a mutual adaptation of candidates to voters and vice versa would be observed.

The creation of political groups is an unusual task to set collaborative filtering, and in order to perform it the technology will need to be modified. However, the underlying principle of establishing the proximity of people from the similarity of their experience and preferences is unchanged. In all the spheres for applying collaborative filtering which we have looked at up till now the talk was of "experience goods", badly categorised and which it is simpler and cheaper to experience than to try working out what they amount to. A major consideration when choosing is taste. We might think political figures have a lot in common with experience goods, but they do not lend themselves to collaborative filtering. Candidates are hardly the equivalent of works of art, although the sympathies evoked by the screen and poster images in which they are presented to voters are almost decisive in terms of electoral results. Neither are cross recommendations a viable option, where proximity of taste neighbours' preferences in other fields is transferred to politics. At least for the time being it is not clear which similarities could be used to ensure an appropriate transfer, although that is not to say that we may not discover such parallels in the future. To cap it all, if an election is being held there is no time for candidates to be "consumed" and rated by others, enabling their experience to be exploited, as is standard practice in collaborative filtering. Electing a governor or a president is not the same as choosing a book, if only because the act of electing is a one-off and the next attempt is far removed in time.

Another option might be to stitch together groups of politically like-minded people on the basis of their rating of political personalities, but this will not work either because the experience of consuming regional leaders and presidents is one-off and there is little carry over of relevant knowledge. If all electors in their lifetime saw at least a couple of dozen political personalities in the same political role, it might be possible to compile a profile from their ratings which would enable everything to proceed in accordance with the norms of collaborative filtering, but that is not the way things are. It is tempting to try to create a political profile of citizens from their attitude towards particular political events, but these would have to be electors who took a very close interest in political life.

It is, nevertheless, possible to use a modified version of the collaborative method in the political process. This is obvious. The technology is part and parcel of the group economy and can be used to form groups of any description if we choose the right filters. The adaptation needed for politics is that what is needed is not a filtering of preferences (although they can and should be taken into account), but computation of proximity of the criteria people believe should be used to rate candidates. The collaborative system's most basic ability is calculating proximity, and that can be computed on the basis of any assortment of characteristics, including political views.

People could be grouped on the basis of what they want from politicians. Their expectations can be formulated in ordinary, readily comprehensible language, without complicated terminology and beginning with such basic coordinates as "left-right", "socialism-capitalism", "liberalism-statism", "hawk-dove". Suppose a list has been made of what is desired or required of candidates. The voter puts this in order of his personal priorities. It is fine if he chooses to ignore certain attributes, in just the same way that people do not have to have read exactly the same books in order for the system to compute proximity in terms of literature. The list could, for example, include such personal characteristics of the future leader as sex, age, charisma, pragmatism, managerial and political experience. It might include his proposals on financial and economic, social, industrial or fiscal policy. The characteristics could initially be provided by experts, but with time they would be augmented by points identified by voters themselves. This is precisely the way tag navigation on the internet is constructed, which consists of short marker phrases which users attach to particular materials. A user's political profile would be compiled from the priorities he himself had indicated, and then fed in for standard processing by the collaborative algorithm. When a computer programme is calculating the proximity of series of numbers it is entirely indifferent to what the numbers stand for: the rating of art works or political demands. In one case the output will be reference circles based on aesthetic taste, and in the other similar circles of politically like-minded people.

This modification of collaborative filtering is already being used to select consumer goods and services, particularly electronics and hotels. Take as an example the choice of a professional camera. The major considerations here are not only taste preferences, but also pragmatic aspects like price, the purposes for which and the conditions under which photographs are expected to be taken. The best advisers will be purchasers who were guided by the same considerations. It is, of course, also extremely helpful to discover what kind of considerations these were. It is from these people that the reference group should be drawn which will advise the user, and with which he will have the opportunity of socialising.

This variety of collaborative filtering is also suitable for searching for professional literature, a task which to this day is coped with incredibly badly. When selecting proximate advisers, priority should be given not to past ratings (although that information is not irrelevant), but to the criteria the potential taste neighbour currently employs in selection. The publications may be cutting edge or popular, may attract readers by the style of their exposition or their interesting presentation, and may be of interest or not depending on the specific enquiry. The most valuable asset is the experience of people guided by the same considerations.

Using collaborative technologies in politics may have a number of useful spin-offs. For example, they can be used to establish how far a manifesto corresponds to groups' aspirations, all by measuring the proximity of series of numbers which code priorities. This will make it easier for voters to see who they are voting for and why. It will also indicate the gap between the wishes of an individual and the pre-election platform of the activists of a group he is considering joining. There is a temptation to go beyond this and calculate the optimal manifesto – the one which best balances the aspirations of all the groups, – but this is likely to prove fruitless. Kenneth Arrow has shown that in a democracy it is impossible to calculate an optimum of social well-being which would equally satisfy everybody.

What holds out the greatest promise, however, is the fact that in politics as nowhere else it is important to be informed and to have access to informed commentary, key elements of the New Economy. Group filtering throws light on much of what is emerging in the depths of society. The willingness of a person to join a particular group or party is directly affected by knowing how other people are reacting to information, and knowing their intentions. This is precisely the way we weigh up the prospects of a particular association. Election results depend not only on what people have heard about candidates and been told in their statements. No less important is whether they know who other people are going to vote for, and what considerations they are guided by. An admirably conceived group will not become popular if it does not show the requisite pace of growth. Good dynamic characteristics are in themselves a catalyst for voters.

Publicly available information about potential supporters of particular initiatives is decisive in determining the viability of civil and political associations. Before attempting to implement anything or joining any group, it is advisable to weigh up the likelihood of its attracting a sufficient number of supporters. Without that, all efforts will be wasted. An initiative may fail to take off, not because nobody is interested but purely because potential supporters are too dispersed. No business-like initiative can afford not to attract the necessary social backing. The autocrats of old Russia were well aware of this secret and throughout Russian history kept socially active groups divided. When the favourites of the tsars were rewarded with lands, their patrimonies were scattered over an enormous area to prevent their owners acquiring a local power base.

A mechanism publicising the rallying of society around particular initiatives will substantially raise the meaningfulness and quality of political processes. The internet with its communicative capabilities offers excellent tools to do just this. It is merely a matter of making use of them. For this rules and procedures are needed to make it possible to collect well thought out, responsible proposals from people wishing to participate in a particular project. Responsibilities should be allocated on a basis of being well informed, that is, having the ability to take account of other people's intentions. Requirements for choosing knowledgeably include:

- A comprehensible explanation of all proposals, including the cost of supporting them. This is needed to enable each individual to choose for himself what is most important and to direct his efforts intelligently;
- Information about the minimum essential or optimal number of supporters required to make the project feasible and able to start;

– Information online about the rate of increase of the number of people expressing a provisional intention of joining, and the "cost" of participating given the numbers currently listed.

It is critically important to state these conditions plainly and to make clear the moment at which a membership application assumes the form of a binding contract. Collaborative filtering is ideally suited to coping with these tasks, especially where it is desirable to know not only how many have signed up but also to have a deeper knowledge of who they are. If this kind of practice were adopted it would complicate the game of politics, but there is no simpler way apparent for balancing interests against each other without crushing any of the groups.

Two further important functions for the collaborative space are a 24/7 feedback channel for voters' opinions, and a spokesperson for the feedback. Thus, a dynamic rating and reputation can be derived for the person eventually elected based on the online ratings of citizens which indicate how far actual policy is corresponding to pre-electoral promises. (This is clearly a threat for politicians.) It is also plain that collaborative filtering is a two-edged sword: knowing the views of the public may make it easier to pander to them. However, the strength of the institution is that (a) leaders will have to compete openly; (b) they will not be able to control a multi-million social arbiter.

Chapter 4
Conclusion

The mission of the modern economy is to create conditions which enable people to develop their individuality in accordance with their wishes and abilities, while at the same time enabling them, despite all their differences, to live together. A system of groups is not some secondary element of one's lifestyle, but a fundamental means of enabling each person to realise himself in a circle of like-minded people, while simultaneously localising effects which might be negatively perceived outside the boundaries of that community. In this sense a group-based organisation of life is the most liberal means of balancing the interests of the individual and society. It provides an opportunity, amongst other things, of avoiding the uniformity in everyone and everything which is the direction in which we are nudged by the profit motive with its enthusiasm for standardising products. This is why so much attention has been paid in this book to the institutional development of a group system, which should move in three directions.

The first is ideological. Just as an individual may be unhappy mainly because he fails to see or does not appreciate his strengths, so it is damaging for a society to be at odds with its own nature and the overall direction in which it is developing. Many have a negative view of the New Economy and underestimate its humane potential. To understand the parameters within which change is occurring is already half the battle.

The second is as a method by which society may better understand itself. All the requisite elements are present to enable us to measure symbolic exchange quantitively and analyse the dissemination of information. These investigations will make it possible to rescue humanitarian thought and practice from its present state of stagnation.

The third is practical. Everything is in place for the introduction of new standards of behaviour which will facilitate self-realisation and increase high-quality personal

A. Dolgin, *Manifesto of the New Economy*,
DOI 10.1007/978-3-642-21277-2_4, © The Author(s) 2012

time. This is what group filtering, the technology of information-based interaction between people, serves. It is based on reflecting on personal experience and providing straightforward access to the experience of others, primarily fellow group members. This tool enables a person to see for himself the connection between the efforts he makes and the results achieved. It enables him to manage change (including change in himself) at a fundamentally different level. Modern man cannot be said to be averse to self-observation and self-analysis. Rather, he often wallows in introspection. This kind of self-contemplation is, however, not all that is needed for the valid feedback which underlies any purposeful development, including personal development. A link showing efforts input and resultant output is always provided in professional and economic activity but almost never when it is 'only' a matter of oneself. This blind spot is so customary that people are not aware of or disquieted by it. In the past the snag was that documentation and self-monitoring entailed high psychological and time costs. These were tedious occupations which required pedantry on an almost perverse scale. The keeping of diaries, in particular, was not for everyone. Automated group filtering has made the process easy and widely available.

Already in the period of Web 2.0, documented self-observation with varying degrees of detail became an everyday habit. The transition to Web 3.0 introduces a qualitative change. Reflection acquires an ideal, digital form which makes it possible to resolve a great variety of urgent problems, from raising the efficiency of consumer choice to taking proper account of personal time. A minimum effort is called for, but no more than is involved in playing a game.

The transformation of useful but hitherto not widespread techniques into a routine is a revolutionary process, despite its apparent banality. To take an example from military history: Maurice, the son of William of Orange, created a major innovation almost out of nothing. He modernised the system for training soldiers, introducing a step-by-step refinement of fighting techniques. For example, the procedure for loading a musket was broken down into several dozen standardised movements. This might not seem particularly novel – the musket was still a musket – but such is the delight of social innovations which have stood the test of time. They appear simple, even banal, but yield astonishing results. The speed of fire and effectiveness of the Orange army increased several times over. Committed to training, the soldiers ceased to go out of their minds from boredom and became less likely to mutiny. They became used to drill and developed a sense of social solidarity which ensured coordinated action even under the extreme conditions of battle. These accompanying effects almost eclipsed the original reason for introducing them. Something similar is to be expected with collaborative filtering.

High achievement is half a matter of firmly establishing routines, whether in sport, education, creativity or elsewhere. If people systematically register the quality of their inner time, that too will improve before our eyes.

The observation has been made on more than one occasion that the increase in idleness in materially prosperous countries and social strata makes the problem of finding something to do extremely urgent. A way needs to be found of engaging human activity, as far as possible non-productively, so that no one loses their job and as little damage is done as possible. One of the most promising approaches has been to redirect concern to the matter of personal time. If we devote the same amount of time to this as we currently do to worrying about our health, a vast realm of activity will open up, complete with its own laws and prospects.

One possible anxiety needs to be dealt with straight away. Collaborative filtering increases society's economic efficiency, reduces costs of the traditional scheme of distribution, and thereby abolishes a certain number of jobs. This flatly contradicts the New Economy's mission of ensuring universal busyness. Economising on social costs could indeed have negative consequences if there were not a large number of niches waiting to take up the slack. The New Economy with its production and supplying of social games provides a global space able to absorb any amount of human energy. Since these games matter, it is important to further develop their rules. Automating the thinking about quality time and people collaborating in the processing of information are serious improvements to the rules and make the game more rigorous, complex and interesting.

It is important not to regard rules and institutions as something static, unchallengeable and set in aspic. Rules can and must be renewed, and so must the human beings governed by them. People, as we know from history, are infinitely plastic and responsive to external motivation. Within living memory they have shown their best qualities, and there have been other occasions when they sank to a subhuman level. A person with his values and habits is not something unchanging. He is shaped by the circumstances in which he lives, including standards and values inherited from the past. There is an academic debate about which should have primacy, the individual or social institutions. Which of these leads and which is led is decided through action. To some extent, the rules can be influenced directly, but the individual only by means of new rules. Changes may begin with a recognition of new values, for example the value of personal time. This is something the collaborative system with its toolbox for registering and reflecting the quality of time facilitates. Before you know it there will be a move to new rules and standards.

To conclude, let us point out a drawback associated with the transition to second (gratuity) money. The innovation has plenty of risks which cannot be fully anticipated while standing on the riverbank. Today people complain about the excessive power of money and the undervaluation of culture, but what if the situation is reversed? With the coming of second money this is entirely possible. If up till now symbolic rivalry between people has been largely covert, when it becomes overt today's capitalist games may seem harmless by comparison. Symbolic domination, quantified and publicly displayed, is a far more powerful irritant than mere material inequality. It is more difficult to resign yourself to the fact that somebody else is cleverer or more talented than you, than to the fact that they are wealthier. This effect is muted by the fact that symbolic capital or talent varies both in accordance with heredity and with the sectors in which it is applied. At least, thanks to the group system, people will not be forced to compete on someone else's territory under rules they are not comfortable with.

People assess economic inequality and tension in a society by the difference in income between the haves and have-nots. The comparison tends to be made between the income of the top 10% and the bottom 10% of the social scale. When some time in the future that gulf is measured in terms of symbolic capital, it will become glaringly obvious how great the danger is. Let us hope that the emergence of markets of personal time will do more good than bad. Society is capable of adapting to such challenges, as to all the other difficulties which only stimulate its development. It will be able to divide itself without undue friction into those who are players in the game and the rest who are not. The new group economy will see to that. Thanks to its contribution the symbolic field is constantly expanding and becoming better ordered, so that anybody who wants to find a place in it, can.

Appendices

Empirical Data Extracted from a Collaborative System[1]

A collaborative site can be used as an experimental space for the social sciences. In the Appendices examples are given of how data can be extracted from internet sites and the kind of questions they enable us to answer. First we look at statistics which accumulate on any site where users are invited to rate something. Such functionality is to be found on all Web 3.0 sites, and a number of second-generation websites. Although a serious drawback of the latter is anonymisation, so that it is impossible to trace what a particular individual has rated, users' responses do have a certain value.

It seems logical to begin with general rules, for example, with the picture of distribution of users' ratings as a whole, over all sectors of consumption, and then to move on to breakdowns of product segments, genres, and the socio-demographic characteristics of consumers. The relevant tables will be found below.

[1]Research was conducted jointly with the Imhonet analysts A. Lebedev and I. Zakharov.

A. Dolgin, *Manifesto of the New Economy*,
DOI 10.1007/978-3-642-21277-2, © The Author(s) 2012

Ratings Distribution on Imhonet

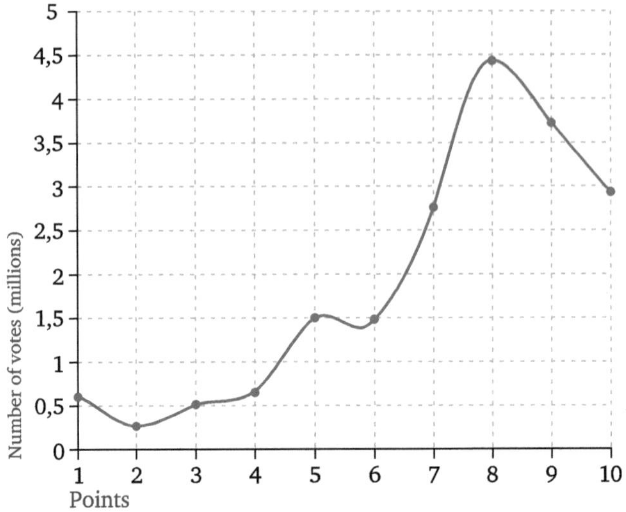

The first striking feature is the high average, and the even higher most frequent rating of '8' (See Table). For commercial culture to meet its audience's expectations so successfully is unexpected, although it may result from adaptation of demands and expectations to the level of supply. There is also the consideration that human memory tends to retain good memories and to block out those less agreeable. This might result in incomplete registering of the latter.

Appendix 1: The Law of Conservation of Happiness: Empirical Data

When moving from the overall ratings distribution to distribution by kinds of consumption, a curious feature is that users overall rate different products similarly. The frequency with which points on the scale are awarded corresponds to a so-called Gaussian distribution (a bell-shaped curve), with the peak always in the region of '8'. The ratings distribution for the cinema is the same as for computer games, brands, or deodorants. Whichever area we look at, literature (all genres), websites, blogs, music or wines, the Tables are all but identical (except for television: something which merits separate analysis).

Ratings Distribution in Various Areas of Consumption

Movies

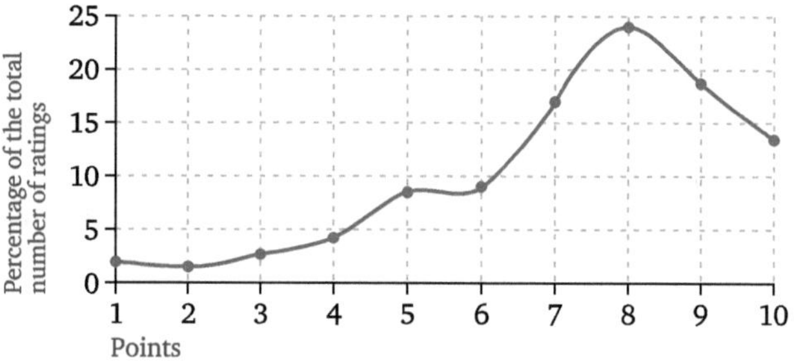

Literature

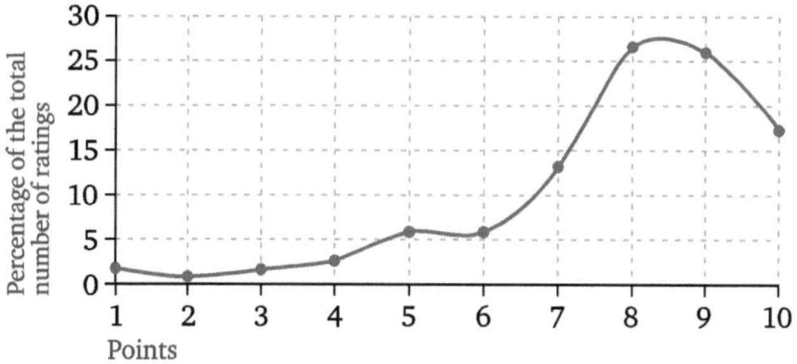

Music

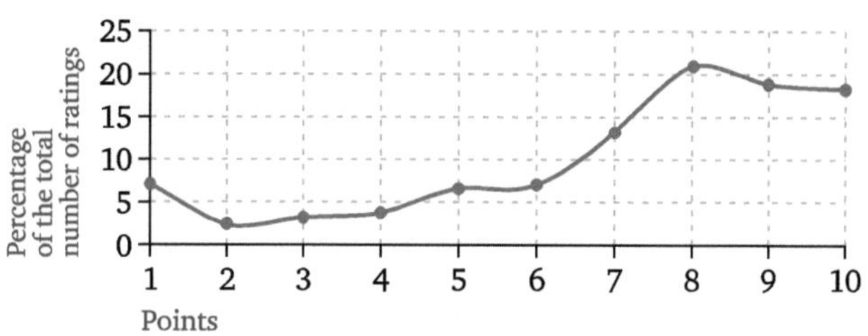

Games

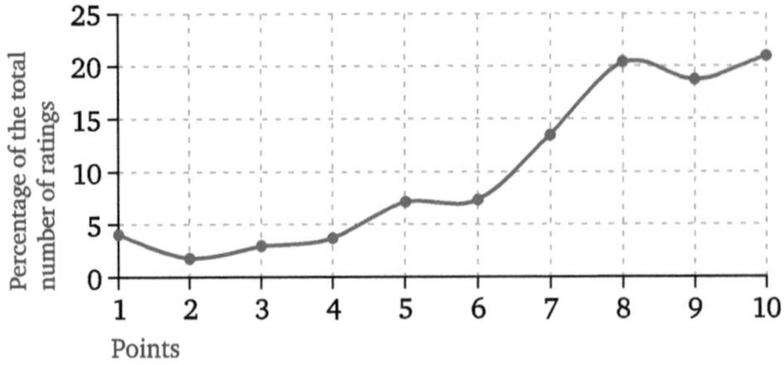

Websites

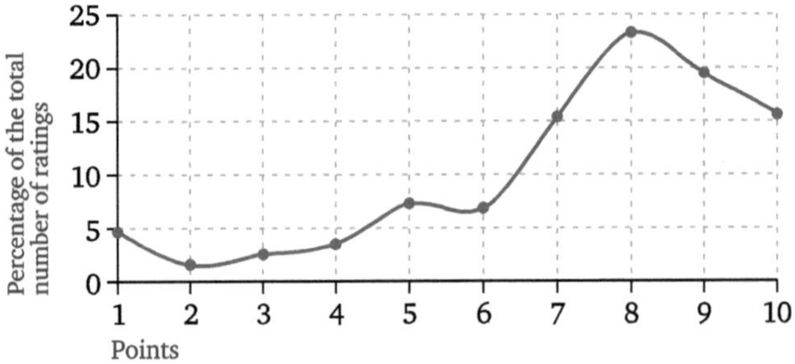

TV

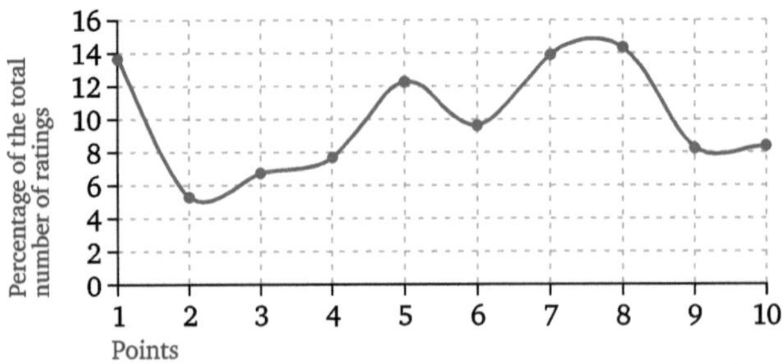

Distribution of Ratings by Type of Consumption: Overall Picture

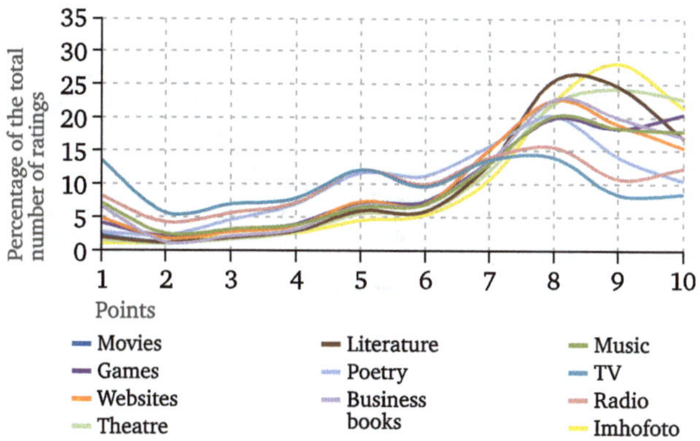

If we move from cultural to socio-demographic cross-sections, we find the same distribution curves. Ratings of consumer satisfaction awarded by women are identical to those awarded by men, and the ratings of young people do not differ from those of adults except that, anomalously, children award many '10's. This is readily explicable.

Overall Ratings Distribution on Imhonet

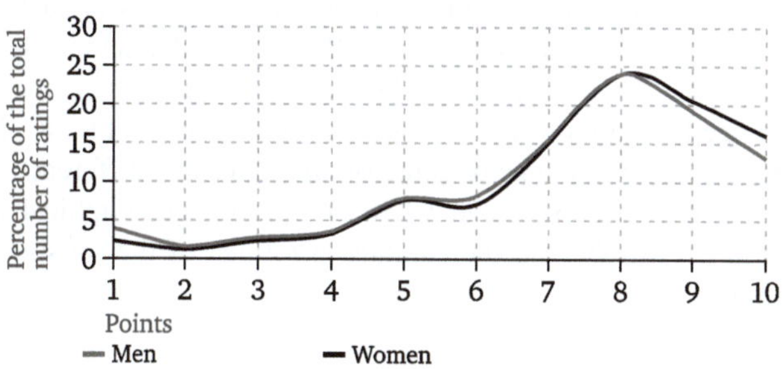

Ratings Distribution by Imhonet Sections

Distribution for Literature

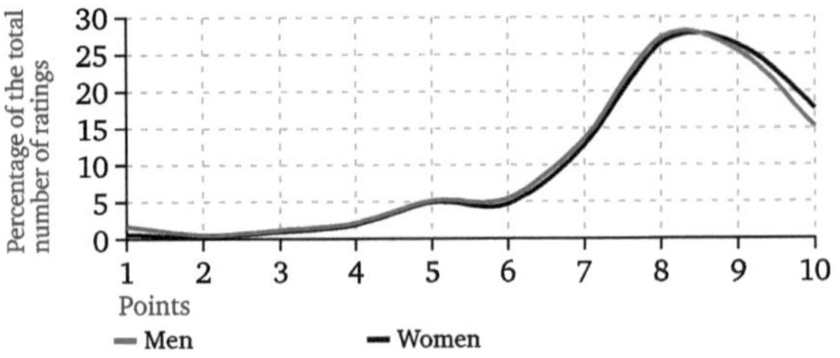

Distribution for Movies

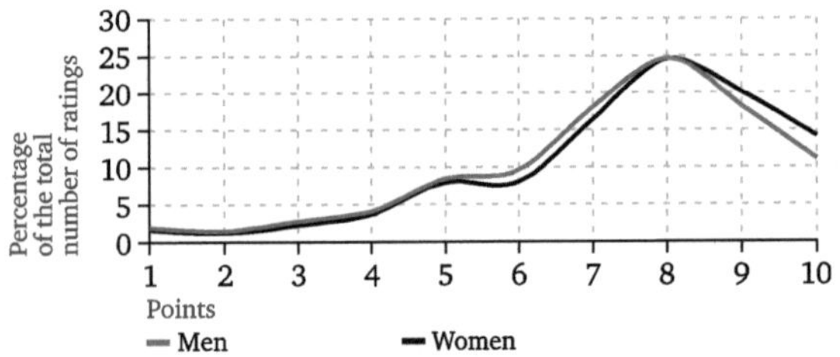

Such admirable consistency in the distribution of ratings is spellbinding, but prompts us to seek an approach to discover differences. All attempts, however, lead to the same results. No matter which breakdowns are chosen, the distribution remains unchanged, with its peak hovering inexorably above the '8'. Neither age, sex, taste preferences nor the type or genre of art makes any difference whatsoever. Neither are differences to be found when comparing geographical regions: the provinces are in no way behind the capitals in ratings of the satisfaction of their cultural requirements.

Ratings Distribution by City

Moscow

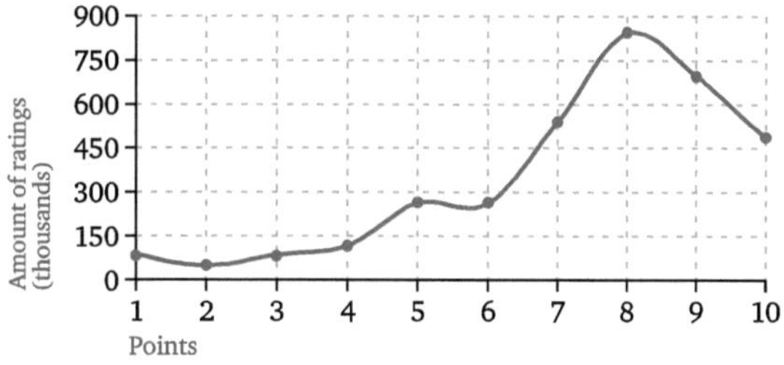

St Petersburg

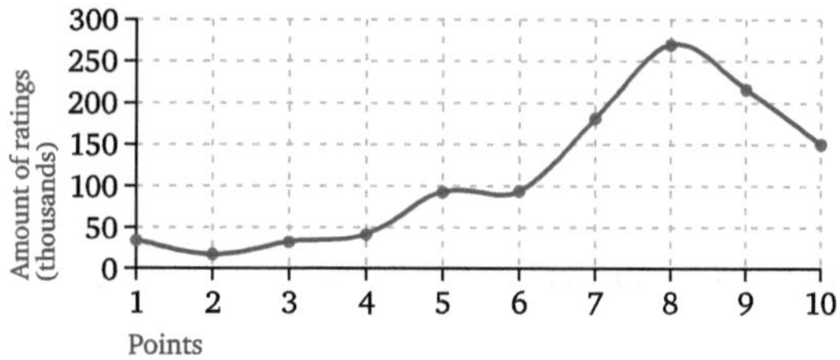

Kiev

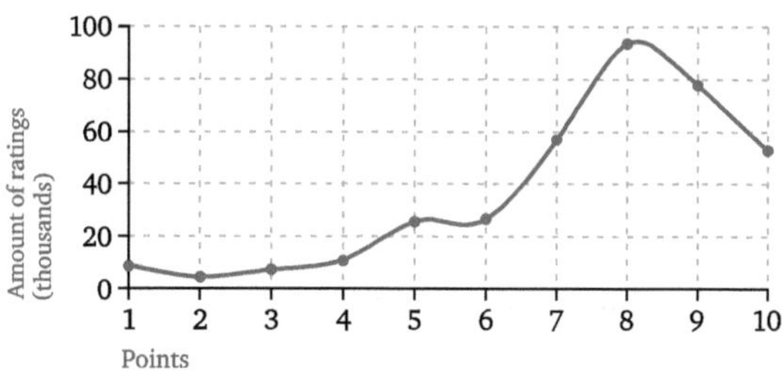

Novosibirsk

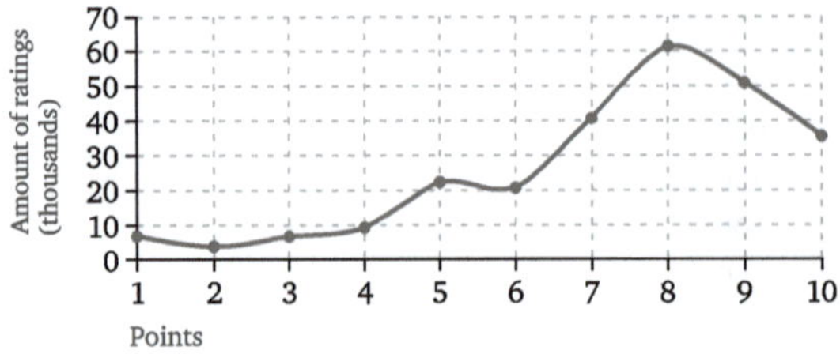

Yekaterinburg

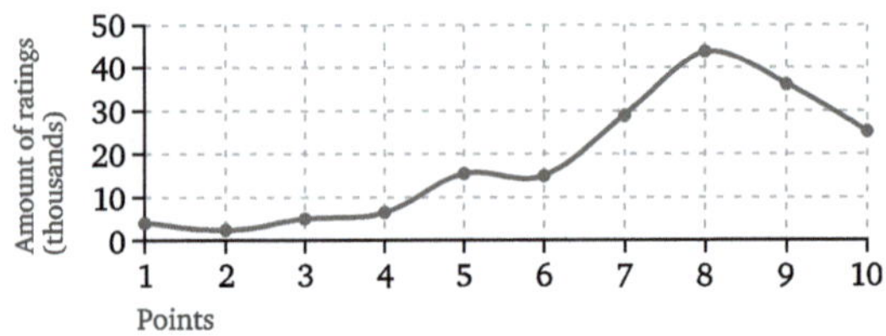

Summary Ratings Distribution by City

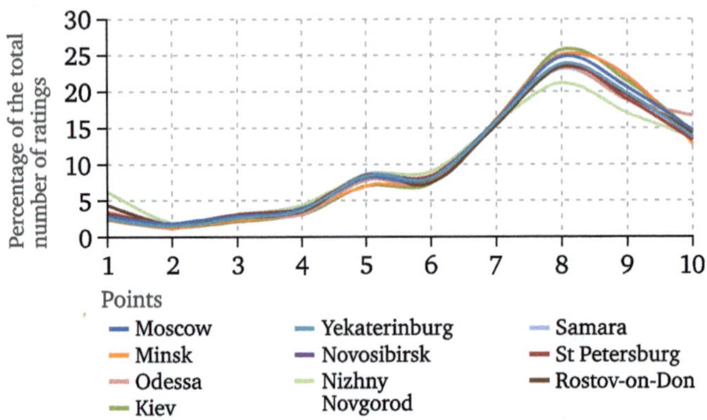

Thus, no matter how ingeniously we probe, the distribution remains identical. This rather unexpected result may indicate something fundamental about the organisation of the human brain. We appear to have stumbled upon an anthropological 'emotional constant'.

It appears, that people get their own dosage of pleasure independently of the quality level or parameter of the product, which they can afford. (As physical bodies, independently of their volume, drop down at the same pace.) The emotional capability is structured in such a way that whatever the quality of a cultural product is like, man chooses his own standard of pleasure. (In principle this observation is of grave consequences, as it could serve as justification to reduce the quality of life.) After deviating from the the accustomed quality level a certain time is needed to adapt again, after which a person will establish his standard anew, in other words, he will again regain his capability of deriving pleasure as he used to do before. It goes without saying, that this does not imply that different people have one and the same feeling with the same emotional fever. However, on the whole there is no perceptible difference, as there is nothing which could function as calibrating standard or as unit of emotional strength (as we don't know to what extent certain pain really hurts another human being). Everybody builds his feeling of content according to the affordable parameter of perception, and the corresponding assortment of products and services. And if the latter is narrowed, the emotion diagram will not record any noticeable changes. These empirical data work in favour of the „pursuit of happiness" law (see chapter 3. 2. The Un/happiness Economics).

Appendix 2: Consumer Typology of Movies

We give below an example of a different kind of information derived from social networks: the classification of movies based on cinemagoers' ratings.

These ratings distribution Tables demonstrate averaged rating and a flat ratings distribution, or, in common parlance, the extent to which spectators are unanimous in awarding a particular rating. (In mathematical statistics this is called the standard deviation or dispersion).

Taking the average rating as a basis, we can clearly distinguish three categories of movies:

1–3: low-rated movie (the closer to 1, the worse the movie);
4–6.3: averagely rated;
6.4–10: highly rated (if the average point score is above 7.9, this generally indicates an outstanding movie).

In respect of averagely rated movies the following varieties of curves are observed: uniform (flat), polar (bimodal), and standard.

From the dispersion of ratings we can identify three gradations:

1–2: flat distribution (indicates unanimity of rating);
2–2.5: typical distribution;
2.5–5 diffuse distribution. Can be uniform or polar.

Categories which movies can be allocated, based on their average rating and dispersion

Very Highly Rated Movie (Average Point 7.9–8.7), Flat Rating Distribution (Dispersion 1.7–2.2)

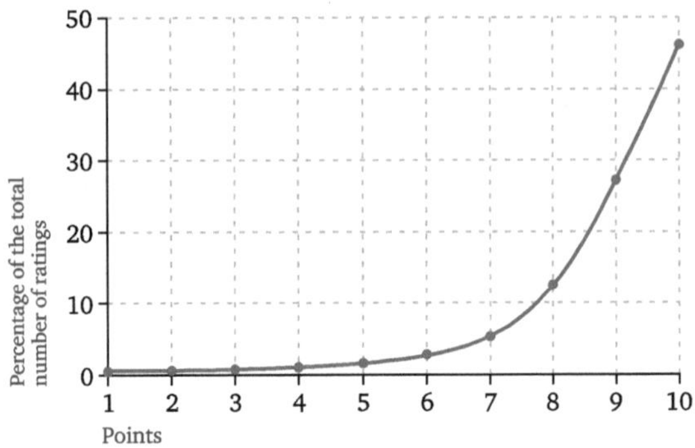

This distribution is typical of outstanding movies which have either already entered the cinema's Hall of Fame or have cast iron claims to do so. Examples are:

Western serials ('Doctor House', No. 8; see Table);
Art movies ('The Outskirts'), No. 6; 'Paris, je t'aime', No. 14);
Russian blockbuster ('The island', No. 7);
Universally beloved Soviet movie ('An office romance', No. 2);
Universally adored cartoon ('Last year's snow was falling', No. 3).

No	Title	Year	Country	Movie's budget ($)	Box-office takings, worldwide, $	Average rating	Standard deviation of ratings
Landmark Soviet cinema							
1	«Ivan Vasilievich changes profession»	1973	USSR			8.6	1.7
2	«An office romance»	1977	USSR			8.5	1.8
3	«Last year's snow was falling»	1983	USSR			8.8	1.6
4	«Heart of a dog»	1988	USSR			8.7	1.7
Landmark Russian cinema							
5	«Cloud paradise»	1991	Russia			8.1	1.9
6	«The outskirts» (art movie)	1998	Russia			8.2	1.9
7	«The island»	2006	Russia	1,500,000	2,495,328	8.2	1.9
Landmark Western serials							

(continued)

No	Title	Year	Country	Movie's budget ($)	Box-office takings, worldwide, $	Average rating	Standard deviation of ratings
8	«House, M.D. (2004–2009)»	2004	USA			8.8	1.7
Box-office success blockbusters							
9	«Forrest Gump»	1994	USA	55,000,000	677,386,686	8.6	2.0
10	«Snatch»	2000	USA/UK	10,000,000	83,557,872	8.4	1.7
11	«A beautiful mind»	2001	USA	58,000,000	313,542,341	8.4	1.6
12	«Love actually»	2003	UK/USA	40,000,000	244,931,766	8.3	1.9
13	«The notebook»	2004	USA	29,000,000	115,533,700	8.5	1.7
Art movies							
14	«Paris, je t'aime»	2006	France/UK	16,000,000	17,335,978	8.2	1.7
15	«Wall-E»	2008	USA	180,000,000	521,268,237	7.9	2.2
Box-office flops							
	«Dead man»	1995	USA	9,000,000	1,037,847	8.4	1.8
17	«Across the universe»	2007	USA	70,000,000	29,367,143	8.2	1.9

Highly Rated Movie (6.4–8.2), Standard Ratings Distribution (Dispersion 1.5–2.4)

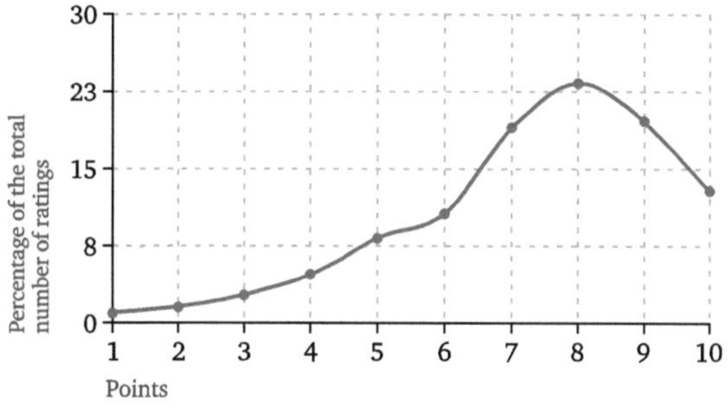

High-quality, successful movies which readily find an audience. Examples are:

Low-budget, box-office success, Western blockbuster ('Lost in translation', No. 19 in the Table);
High-budget, box-office success Western blockbuster ('The dark knight', No. 23);
Successful Russian blockbuster ('Brother', No. 3);
Multi part Russian movie ('Admiral', No. 13; 'The liquidation', No. 6);

Soviet (or Russian) multi-part movie or Russian soap opera ('The master and Margarita', No. 2);
Art movie ('The return', No. 12);
Oscar-winning box-office success blockbuster ('Wanted', No. 24; 'Slumdog millionaire', No. 25; 'Juno', No. 26);
Low-budget, box-office success movie ('Open water', No. 16).

No	Title	Year	Country	Movie's budget ($)	Box-office takings, worldwide,$	Average rating	Standard deviation of ratings
Russian multi-part movies							
1	«The idiot»	2003	Russia			8.2	1.7
2	«The master and Margarita»	2005	Russia	5,000,000		7.4	2.2
Low-budget entertainment Russian movies							
3	«Brother»	1997	Russia			7.7	2.0
4	«Brother –2»	2000	Russia	1,500,000	1,080,000	7.5	2.0
5	«The Turkish gambit»	2005	Russia	4,000,000	18,500,000	7.2	1.9
6	«The liquidation»	2007	Russia			8.1	1.7
7	«The cuckoo»	2002	Russia	4,000,000	554,763	7.8	1.6
8	«Bastards»	2005	Russia	2,500,000	9,662,55	6.4	2.4
9	«Piter FM»	2006	Russia	1,000,000	7,242,206	7.3	2.1
10	«Wild field»	2008	Russia			7.4	1.8
11	«Night watch»	2004	Russia	4,200,000	33,851,015	6.0	2.5
Art movies							
12	«The return»	2003	Russia	400,000	4,047,830	8.2	1.7
Russian blockbusters							
13	«Admiral»	2008	Russia	20,000,000	38,135,878	6.8	2.4
14	«Hipsters»	2008	Russia	15,000,000	16,806,500	6.9	2.4
15	«August 1944»	2001	Russia / Belarus	5,052,780		8.0	1.5
Low-budget, box-office success films							
16	«Open water»	2003	USA	500,000	54,667,954	6.5	2.2
17	«Brokeback mountain»	2005	USA	14,000,000	178,043,761	7.1	2.5
Western blockbusters							
18	«The big Lebowski»	1998	USA	15,000,000	17,451,873	7.5	2.1
19	«Lost in translation»	2003	USA	4,000,000	119,723,856	7.0	2.2
20	«The Da Vinci code»	2006	USA	125,000,000	758,239,851	6.5	2.2
21	«Die hard 4»	2007	USA	110,000,000	383,531,541	7.2	2.0
22	«What happens in Vegas»	2008	USA	35,000,000	219,252,257	7.2	2.0

(continued)

No	Title	Year	Country	Movie's budget ($)	Box-office takings, worldwide,$	Average rating	Standard deviation of ratings
23	«The dark knight»	2008	USA	185,000,000	1,001,921,825	7.5	2.2
24	«Wanted»	2008	USA	75,000,000	341,433,252	6.7	2.2
25	«Slumdog millionaire»	2008	USA / UK	15,000,000	377,417,293	7.8	2.0
26	«Juno»	2007	USA / Canada / Hungary	7,500,000	231,404,554	7.4	1.8
27	«Perfume: the story of a murderer»	2006	France/Spain/ Germany	60,000,000	135,039,924	7.5	2.0
28	«Babel»	2006	France/USA/ Mexico	25,000,000	135,330,163	7.6	1.9

Averagely Rated Movie (Average 4.7–6.0), Standard Ratings Distribution (Dispersion 2.1–2.6)

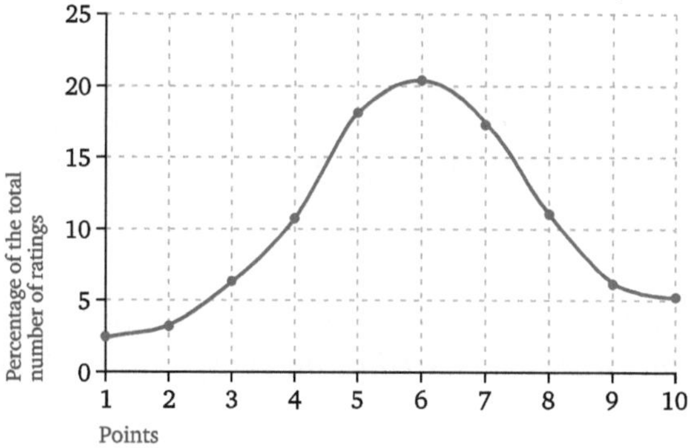

If the rating is around '5', or somewhat lower, this suggests a mediocre movie in every respect, which the majority of cinemagoers either did not much enjoy or which rather disappointed them. The distribution fate of such movies depends on advertising: the budget and effectiveness of promotion lead ultimately to box office success or failure. Examples:

A box-office success Russian movie ('Heat', No. 6 in the Table);
High-budget Russian flop ('The inhabited island', 2 parts, Nos. 9–10);
High-budget Western flop ('Solaris', No. 17).

No	Title	Year	Country	Movie's budget ($)	Box-office takings, worldwide,$	Average rating	Standard deviation of ratings
Russian movies							
1	«Bummer»	2003	Russia	700,000	1,600,000	6.0	2.4
2	«Deadly force»	2003	Russia			5.6	2.4
3	«Shadow boxing»	2005	Russia	3,500,000	8,262,833	5.9	2.3
4	«180 and over»	2005	Russia		1,274,435	6.1	2.0
5	«Heat»	2006	Russia	5,550,000	15,710,000	4.8	2.5
6	«Gloss»	2007	Russia	2,500,000	4,684,165	5.6	2.2
7	«Apocalypse code»	2007	Russia	15,000,000	10,446,654	4.7	2.4
8	«An irony of fate: the sequel»	2007	Russia	5,000,000	55,635,037	5.5	2.6
9	«Inhabited island: part 1»	2008	Russia	36,500,000	21,834,845	5.4	2.6
10	«Inhabited island: part 2»	2009	Russia		6,069,159	5.2	2.5
Successful Western movies							
11	«Spy kids 2: island of lost dreams»	2002	USA	38,000,000	119,723,358	5.9	2.2
12	«Hulk»	2003	USA	137,000,000	245,284,946	5.6	2.2
13	«Bewitched»	2005	USA	85,000,000	131,162,908	5.9	2.2
14	«Beowulf»	2007	USA	150,000,000	196,264,091	5.9	2.2
15	«The day the earth stood still»	2008	USA	80,000,000	230,831,978	6.0	2.1
Western flops							
16	«Sky captain and the world of tomorrow»	2004	USA	70,000,000	57,958,696	5.8	2.2
17	«Solaris»	2002	USA	47,000,000	30,002,758	6.0	2.2
18	«Babylon A.D»	2008	USA	70,000,000	68,744,968	5.9	2.2

Averagely Rated Movie (Average Rating Around 5), Diffuse Polar (Bimodal) Ratings Distribution (Dispersion More than 2.7)

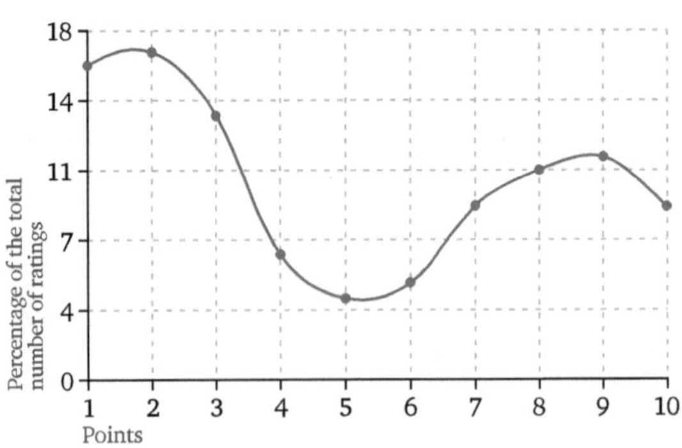

A fairly rare case. Typical of art or mass audience movies dealing with controversial social problems, for example 'Borat'. Such movies are rarely blockbusters. 'Borat' was an exception.

No	Title	Year	Country	Movie's budget ($)	Box-office takings, worldwide,$	Average rating	Standard deviation of ratings
1	«Cop wars»	2005	Russia			5.5	3.2
2	«Borat»	2006	USA	18,000,000	261,507,998	5.3	3.0

Averagely Rated Movie, Diffuse Uniform Ratings Distribution

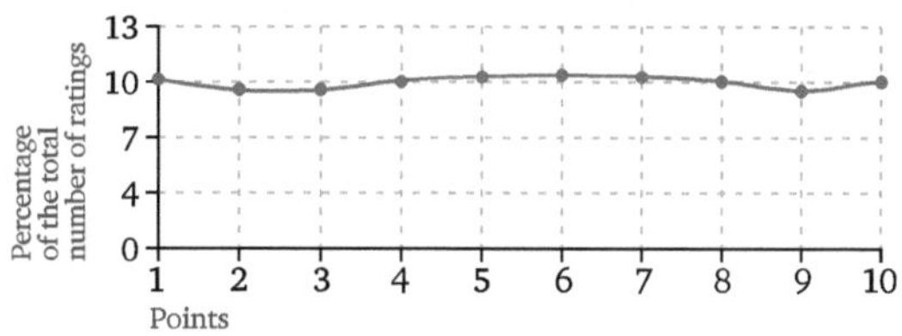

This ratings distribution pattern is typical of blockbusters, which are quite often successful at the box office. This can be ascribed to the merits of a high-budget advertising campaign. Often horror movies. Examples:

Provocative movie ('Brüno', No. 10);
Horror movie ('Saw 5', No. 9).
Russian multi-part movies can also look like this, for example 'The cadets' (No. 3).

No	Title	Year	Country	Movie's budget ($)	Box-office takings, worldwide,$	Average rating	Standard deviation of ratings
Russian serials							
1	«Happy together»	2006	Russia			5.1	2.9
2	«Who wears the trousers?»	2006	Russia			5.3	2.5
3	«The cadets»	2006	Russia			5.6	2.8
Russian blockbuster flops							
4	«The sword bearer»	2006	Russia	5,000,000	3,919,731	5.0	2.6
Western blockbusters							
5	«American pie 2»	2001	USA	30,000,000	287,553,595	5.5	2.7
6		2006	USA	16,000,000	51,685,963	5.3	2.8

(continued)

No	Title	Year	Country	Movie's budget ($)	Box-office takings, worldwide,$	Average rating	Standard deviation of ratings
	«Texas chainsaw massacre: the beginning»						
7	«Scary movie 4»	2006	USA	45,000,000	178,262,620	5.6	2.7
8	«Beverly Hills chihuahua»	2008	USA	20,000,000	149,264,475	5.7	2.8
9	«Saw 5»	2008	USA	10,800,000	113,857,533	5.9	2.8
10	«Bruno»	2009	USA	42,000,000	137,374,387	5.3	2.9

Low-Rated Movie (Average 3.7–4.3), Standard Ratings Distribution (Dispersion 2.2–2.5)

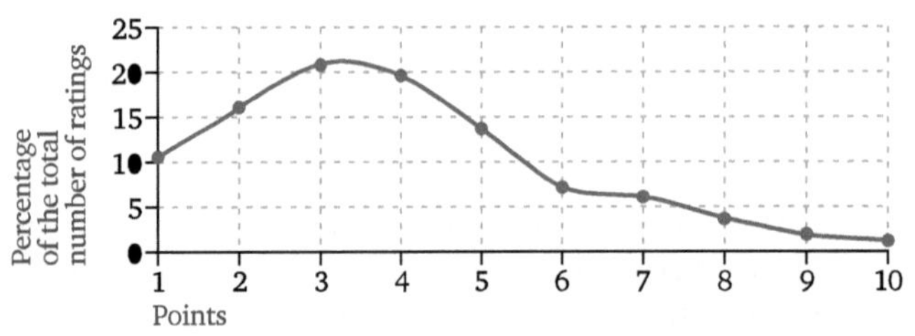

As a rule these are unsuccessful movies of all varieties. For example:

Unsuccessful Russian serial ('Lyuba, the children and the factory', No. 1);
High-budget Russian flop ('Return of the musketeers', No. 4);
High-budget Western flop ('1 million years B.C. 2', No. 6).
Although occasionally there can be box office successes attributable solely to advertising. Such, for example, was the high-budget movie, 'Meet the Spartans' (No. 7).

No	Title	Year	Country	Movie's budget ($)	Box-office takings, worldwide,$	Average rating	Standard deviation of ratings
Russian serial							
1	«Lyuba, the children and the factory»	2005	Russia			3.9	2.3
Russian movie flops							
2	«Tins»	2007	Russia	3,000,000	2,069,986	4.3	2.4
3	«Trackman»	2007	Russia	3,000,000	509,050	3.7	2.2
4		2008	Russia	5,000,000	2,518,449	3.8	2.5

(continued)

No	Title	Year	Country	Movie's budget ($)	Box-office takings, worldwide,$	Average rating	Standard deviation of ratings
	«Return of the musketeers»						
5	«Forbidden Reality»	2009	Russia	7,000,000	1,867,230	3.7	2.3
6	«Artefact»	2009	Russia	5,000,000	281,917	4.2	2.5
Western movie flops							
7	«Beauty and the beast»	2008	USA	9,000,000	1,596,232	3.8	2.4
8	«18 year old virgin»	2009	USA			3.5	2.5
9	«One million years B.C. 2»	2007	France/ Spain	46,000,000	2,173,196	3.8	2.5
Western blockbusters							
10	«Meet the Spartans»	2008	USA	30,000,000	84,646,831	4.1	2.5

Extremely Low-Rated Movie (2.1–3.8), Standard Ratings Distribution, Tending to Diffuse

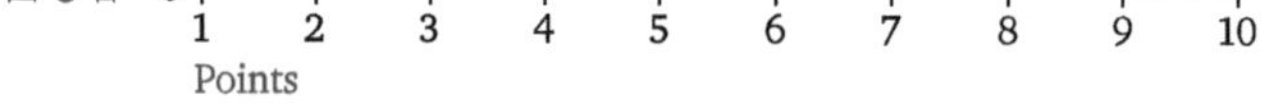

These movies find no audience at all and can be of virtually any kind. A notable representative is the middle-budget flop 'Pledge this!' (No. 4).

It is interesting to compare 'The best movie' and its sequel. Both movies were about equally bad (rating respectively 3.5 and 3.3), but if the former had almost record box-office takings (probably due to the television popularity of the actors in it), in the case of the latter advertising did not yield the earlier return. The movie barely recovered the cost of production.

No	Title	Year	Country	Movie's budget ($)	Box-office takings, worldwide,$	Average rating	Standard deviation of ratings
Non-low-budget (by Russian standards) Russian movie							
1	«The best movie»	2008	Russia	4,500,000	30,496,695	3.5	2.6
2	«Hitler kaputt!»	2008	Russia	3,000,000	9,713,500	3.4	2.5
3	«The best movie 2»	2009	Russia	10,000,000	12,830,025	3.3	2.4
Western flop							
4	«Pledge this!»	2006	USA	20,000,000	1,751,490	2.1	2.2
Very low rating, good box-office takings							
5	«Epic movie»	2007	USA	20,000,000	86,865,564	3.7	2.6
6	«Disaster movie»	2008	USA	20,000,000	34,816,824	3.2	2.6

Appendix 3: Statistics for Russian Movies

In this Appendix we show trends in Russian cinema as evident from cinemagoers' ratings.

Correlation of low, middle, high, and very high ratings of Russian movies over the past six decades

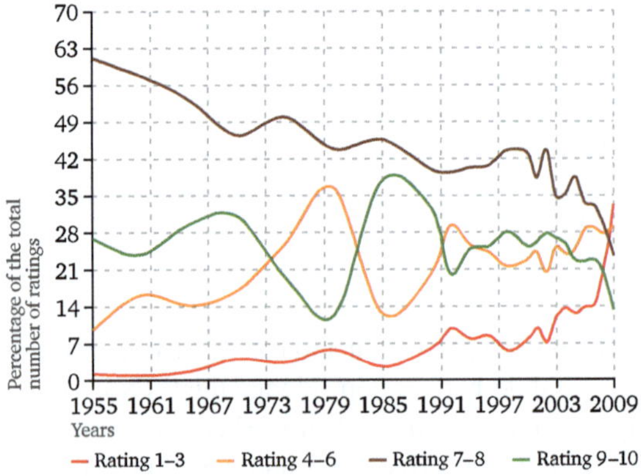

Pattern of Ratings of Russian Cinema: Breakdown by Year

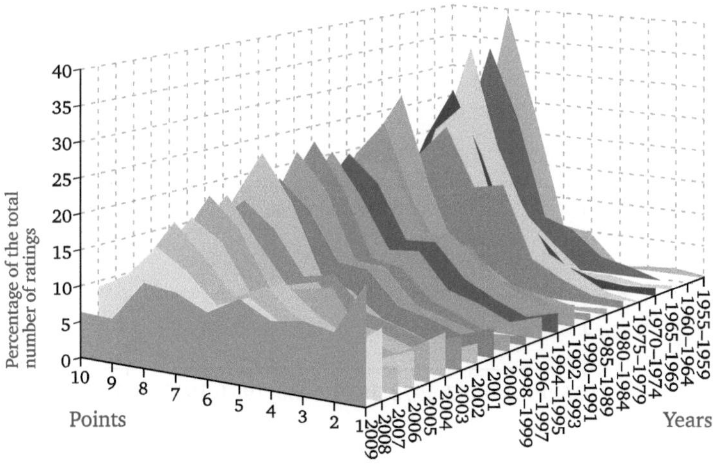

The pattern of curves on the graph might conveniently be called 'the helicopter blade', that is the proportion of high ratings falls over the years, while low ratings grow appreciably. For comparison:

Pattern of Ratings of Western Movies: Breakdown by Year

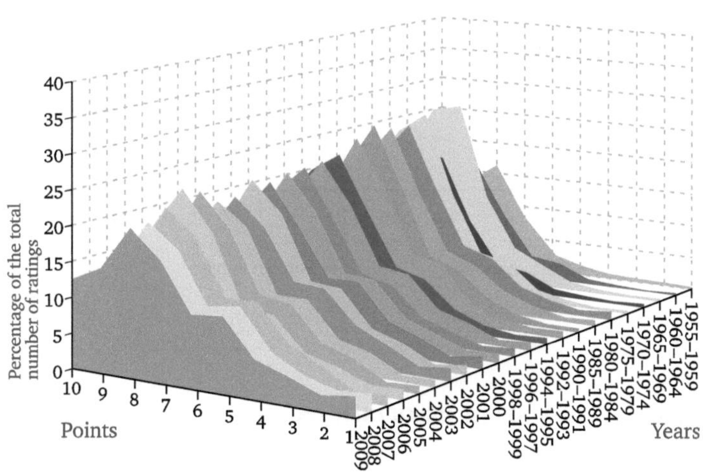

Here the picture is uniform and stable.

Change of the Average Rating of Russian Movies by Year (Based on the Entire Database of Ratings of Russian Movies)

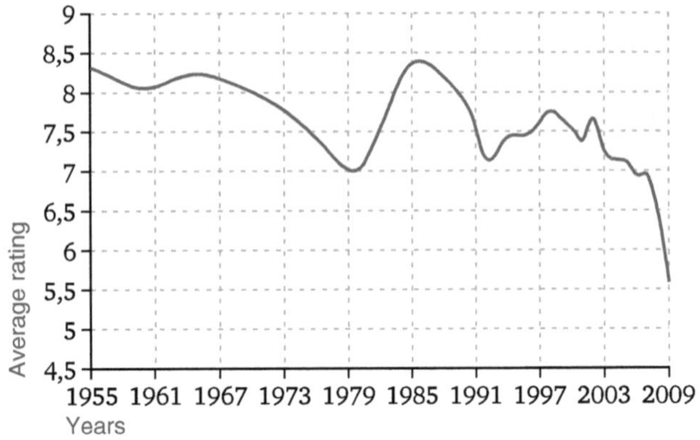

Distribution of Ratings of Russian and Western Movies in 2009

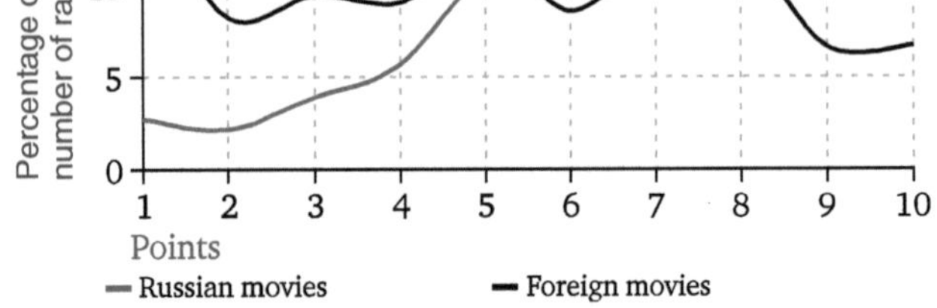

Appendix 4: Analysis of associations

When researching communities it makes sense to focus on the number of communities and how many members they have, the features of their internal structure, the density of links between people, the parameters in accordance with which consolidation occurs, the proximity of certain circles to others, etc. Such matters are most easily discovered with the aid of third-generation networks. Obviously, conventional statistics, including ratings of various kinds, are not suitable for this, primarily because of the anonymity of ratings. In the case of Web 3.0 these problems do not arise because it is evident who is responsible for particular ratings/opinions and who joins which groups. Additional difficulties are created by the 'emotional constant'.

When studying communities it is essential to differentiate potential groups from real ones, that is, those in which communication between participants is already occurring. To the first category belong groups of people who are close to each other in some respect but not yet aware of the fact. A collaborative program detects such links and 'visualises' circles of potential club members. At the same time, various parameters can be taken as the basis. The most obvious is shared interests. For example, a certain number of people prefer a particular genre of literature or a particular kind of holiday. These are potential members of an appropriate club. Another criterion is proximate tastes. Where the two meet a group can be formed with closer ties between people.

For example, more than 1,500 Imhonet users have indicated an interest in playing Mafia, of whom 300 said this was a strong interest. Calculating the taste proximity showed that each of these 300 individuals had on average three 'taste neighbours' from among the other Mafia enthusiasts. We see the same picture if we process data relating to table tennis: more than 4,000 table tennis players are on Imhonet, and of these more than 500 are major enthusiasts. It transpires that for each of these 500 one can choose at least three other users with whom they will find common grounds for socialising outside the sports hall. Accordingly, potential groups are lists of individuals for whom it would in theory be interesting to contact each other because of the proximity of their views, preferences, occupations, tastes, and other coincidences (or, on the contrary, differences – the programme operates with these with equal success).

Groups actually functioning at the present time are the embryos of future larger communities. They are visible to the system through the communications/ transactions between people. The fact that a person belongs to a particular group is determined by the activities in which he participates. It manifests itself both in operations involving the site's directories (awarding ratings, entering new works into the database or the list of 'My interests'), and also in the transactions between users (inclusion in the list of friends, reaction to each other's comments, etc.).

The data below provides an idea of the actions of Imhonet users.

Statistics of User Actions Over the Course of 1 Week

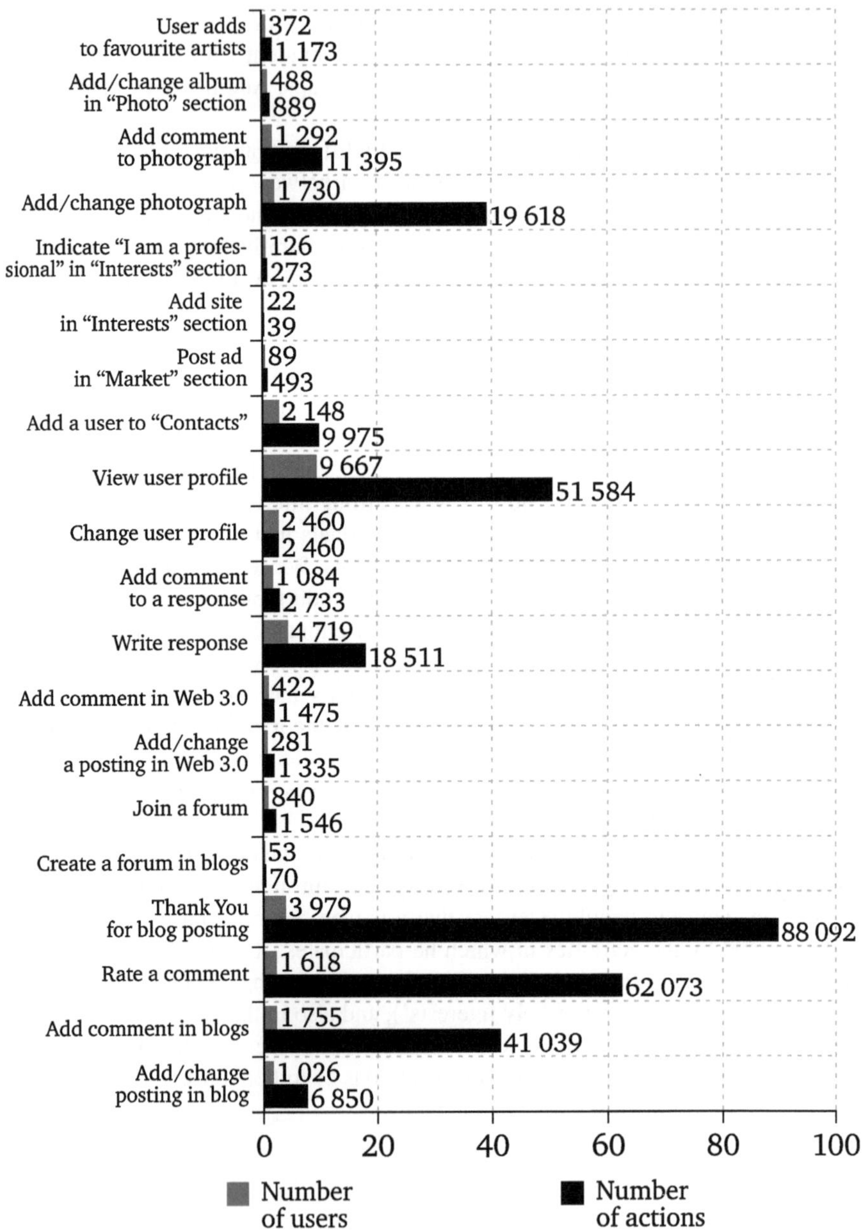

The collaborative system identifies groups, outlining circles of real or potential participants and thereby helping communities in embryo to turn into something definite and viable. For example, a certain community has 1,000 people potentially drawn to it, but at present its nucleus comprises only 15 users. If there are activists who see a prospect of growth, then through their actions they will be able to stimulate others to join: people find it easier to respond when they know they are potential members.

As an example, let us investigate groups in literature, cinema, and music. Users were admitted to one of these groups on two criteria: in the first place, each had to have awarded no fewer than 100 ratings in that particular sector; secondly they had to demonstrate systematic monthly activity testifying to the stability of their interest. A total of several hundred users were selected in each of the areas. Now, what interested us was what quantity of cinemagoers are simultaneously music lovers and/or enjoy reading. The diagram below depicts all the subsets formed by means of intersection of individuals from the three chosen sectors. It will be seen that approximately one-third of all book readers are simultaneously interested in cinema and music.

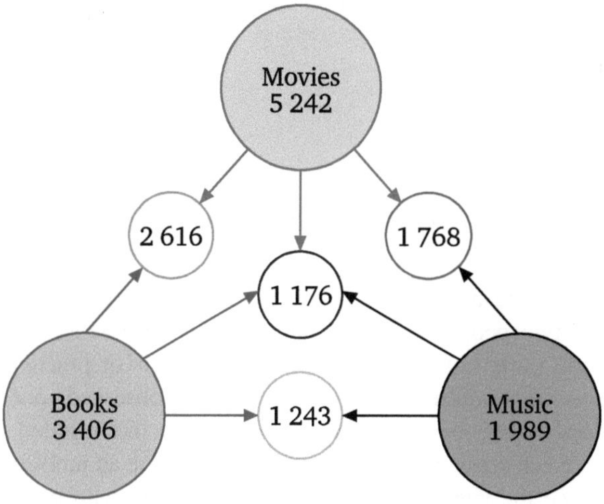

In the following diagram, in the interests of visual clarity, the same thing is depicted in the form of overlapping circles, the size of which is proportionate to the numbers in the corresponding communities.

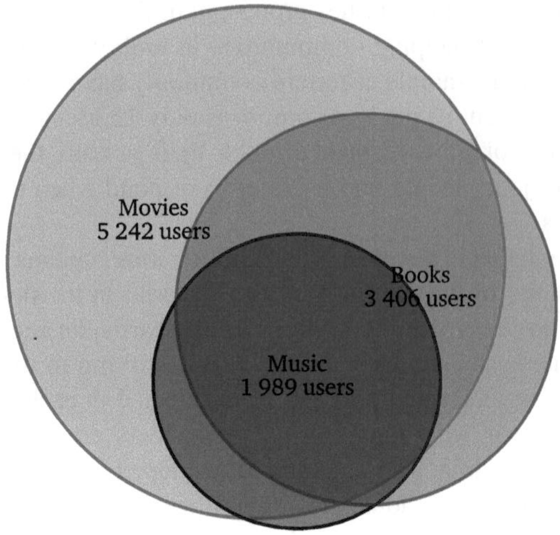

In the same way we can identify communities by genres or movements in literature, the cinema, theatre, through interests in particular kinds of sport, leisure, games (see the Diagram below). We can identify groups on any number of bases and overlapping interests, providing this data is known to the system or has been obtained through calculation.

Examples of Future Projects in the Sphere of Taste

It is curious how closely linked tastes in different areas are to each other. For example, if two people have the same literary preferences, does this mean they will like the same kind of music? The question is of practical significance, since in those sectors where correlation of taste is observed, one can calculate recommendations on the basis of ratings awarded by like-minded people from a different sector. Such cross-cultural recommendations are an innovation introduced on Imhonet. Since the site is working in many areas in parallel, the opportunity arises for 'taste transfers'. This approach is particularly appropriate where it is necessary to recommend something to a newbie in some area, so it is important to know where 'taste transfers' are justified and where they are not. It is a matter of how much or how little a given user's cohort of recommenders changes when he moves from one sector to another. If the overlaps are considerable, cross recommendations are appropriate, but if there is an abrupt change in the composition, they aren't.

The data below relate to recommenders for a user with the nickname of 'Dolgin'. Here is how they interconnect:

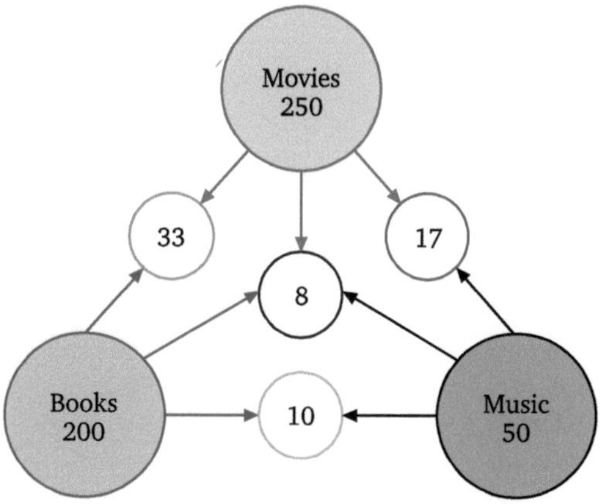

The round figures for the number of users in the reference groups is related to settings in the recommender engine.

The same data in a different graphic form.

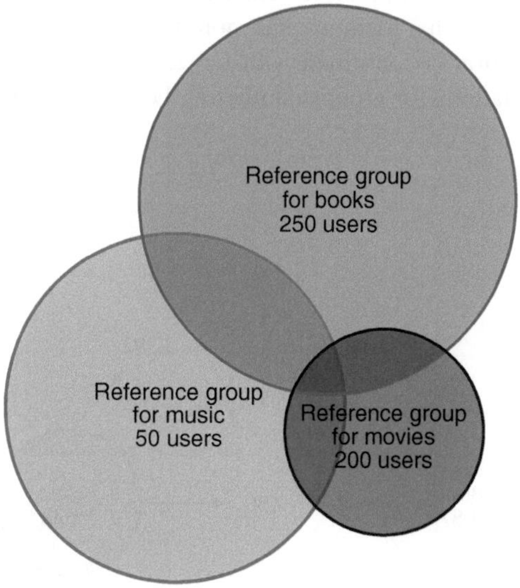

From another, randomly chosen, user (http://temik.imhonet.ru), we obtain a closely similar picture:

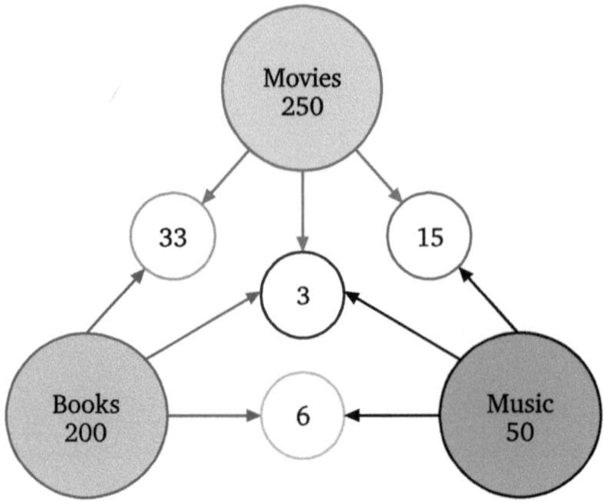

It will be noted that for both users the interconnections of the reference groups in books and music are higher than in movies and music. Consequently, if it is necessary to compute cross-predictions in music, the opinion of like-minded people in the movies section would be more reliable than that of taste neighbours from literature. It is also clear that literature has more in common with movies than with music. This observation is confirmed with larger groups of users. The Diagrams below show computations for groups numbering between 100 and 1,000 users.

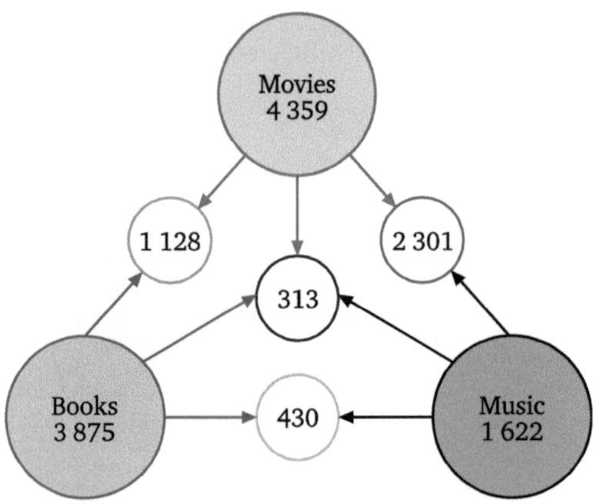

Before we bring down the curtain, let us consider one further matter from the sphere of taste: regarding the differences between admirers of art movies and blockbusters. Both were identified from high ratings of movies in these two categories, and their attitude to prefererred objects of the other group was then analysed. We were just curious to see how blockbuster enthusiasts react to cinema for a narrower audience; and how, on the contrary, aesthetes rate mass culture movies. The results, presented in the Table below, are really very touching. Despite the usually claimed antipathy, art movie devotees like mass culture in exactly the same way as ordinary human beings. This is indicated by a typical curve peaking just above ‘8’. Enthusiasts of thrillers for their part prove even less predictable: their ratings distribution curve for art movies is shifted towards positive assessment even more strongly than that of the aesthetes. They almost all award ‘difficult’ movies ‘10’s. We can only guess what is motivating them more, a desire to present socially acceptable answers, or not to dent their own self-esteem.

Art versus blockbuster. Comparison of ratings of art movies by blockbuster fans and of blockbuster movies by devotees of art movies.

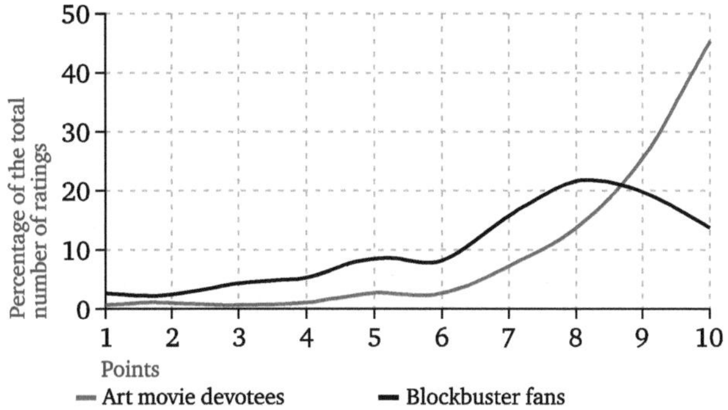

The aim of these Appendices has been to demonstrate on specific examples the kinds of information which can be extracted from third-generation networks and the methods used. In a similar manner answers can be found to an enormous number of other questions. Over to those of you who will ask them.

About the Author

Professor Alexander Dolgin is chairman of the Economics of Culture Department at the National Research University Higher School of Economics. His areas of expertise include the institutional economics of information markets, history and theory of informal institutions, computer science and studies of online social networks. He is also the author of over 200 publications.

Alexander Dolgin is not only an academic, but also a businessman and practitioner who implements the newest business models on the Internet. In his previous book, "The Economics of Symbolic Exchange", he designed and then created Imhonet – a recommendation portal (imhonet.ru), which is an innovative institutional platform for the automated exchange of consumer experiences. Currently, the portal has more than 700,000 users.

A. Dolgin, *Manifesto of the New Economy*,
DOI 10.1007/978-3-642-21277-2, © The Author(s) 2012

MIX
Papier aus verantwortungsvollen Quellen
Paper from responsible sources
FSC® C105338

If you have any concerns about our products,
you can contact us on
ProductSafety@springernature.com

In case Publisher is established outside the EU,
the EU authorized representative is:
Springer Nature Customer Service Center GmbH
Europaplatz 3, 69115 Heidelberg, Germany

Printed by Libri Plureos GmbH
in Hamburg, Germany